Things Your Grammar Never Told You

Things Your Grammar Never Told You

SECOND EDITION

Maurice Scharton
Illinois State University

Janice Neuleib
Illinois State University

New York   San Francisco   Boston
London   Toronto   Sydney   Tokyo   Singapore   Madrid
Mexico City   Munich   Paris   Cape Town   Hong Kong   Montreal

Vice President and Editor-in-Chief: Joseph Opiela
Marketing Manager: Chris Bennem
Supplements Editor: Donna Campion
Production Manager: Ellen MacElree
Project Coordination, Text Design, and Electronic Page
    Makeup: Nesbitt Graphics, Inc.
Cover Design Manager: Nancy Danahy
Cover Designer: Neil Flewellyn
Cover Photo: Copyright© Lara Lepionka
Manufacturing Buyer: Lucy Hebard
Printer and Binder: Webcrafters
Cover Printer: John P. Pow

Library of Congress Cataloging-in-Publication Data

Scharton, Maurice.
    Things your grammar never told you / Maurice
Scharton, Janice Neuleib.—2nd ed.
        p. cm.
    Includes bibliographical references (p.) and index.
    ISBN 0-205-32973-X
    1. English language—Grammar—Handbooks, manuals,
    etc. I. Neuleib, Janice. II. Title.
PE1112.S32 2002
428.2—dc21
                                            2001020385

Please visit our website at http://www.ablongman.com

ISBN 0-205-32973-X

1 2 3 4 5 6 7 8 9 10—WEB—04 03 02 01
                                            3/00

To Phoebe Ann St. Thomas Scharton
and
Sara Irene Smith Witherspoon,
who gave us life and language.

Contents

Preface to the Second Editon

You're working on the final draft of an important writing assignment. You've been staying up all night for a week, living on delivered pizza and instant cappuccino, talking only to spiders. The deadline is six hours away, still plenty of time. Unfortunately, you've gone into brainlock from looking at the comments and symbols on your draft. As far as you were aware, "awk" was the comment of a startled goose and "frag" had to do with hand grenades. So many rules—punctuation, spelling, mechanics, documentation, word choice, sentence structure, not to mention (eek!) grammar—you wish you had a book that would tell you all the *Things Your Grammar Never Told You.*

A happy ending impends because your instructor—a beneficent, providentially, godlike figure—has required you to purchase the second edition of this handbook, chock-full of things your grammar never, ever told you. Some time during the night, the book has fallen to the floor, back pages open to a veritable Neiman-Marcus catalog of writing advice: an explanatory table of grading symbols (including the mystical *awk* and *frag*) near an index and a detailed table of contents. You prop the book next to your computer, which seems to lean affectionately in the book's direction. Investigating more closely, you note the book's abundant cyber-resources: handy computer writing tips scattered strategically through the chapters as well as current APA and MLA citation standards for Web documents, a list of tips for Web page design, and an appendix of online reference sites. Noting the many humorous examples that illustrate the book's advice, you address a nearby spider with your customary understated irony. "Yo, Elwyn, check it out. For a grammar book, this gets an extremely high score on the Flesh-and-Blood Readability Index. And judging from the new sample research paper in APA style, I would guess they've implemented some kind of ethnocentricity filter." Elwyn nods knowingly and scuttles down the page to the list of distinguished teachers, writers, and editors who have advised the authors in preparing the second edition: Lynn Beene, University of New Mexico; Kathleen Bell, University of Central Florida; and Penny Sansbury, Florence-Darlington Technical College.

Reassured, you turn back to your final draft with *Things Your Grammar Never Told You* in hand. Opening to the Preface and Brief Table of Contents, you note the chapter arrangement: sentence structure, word choice, punctuation, spelling and mechanics, and documentation. That looks like a plan. You can work your way through the chapters, using tactics for solving sentence problems, word choice, punctuation, and so on down to the last detail of the last Works Cited page. But you need a proofreading strategy. Elwyn sidles a little farther down the page toward a patch of proofreading advice.

Locate problems and correct them in two separate steps. Use a ruler and pencil (or a highlighter, or check marks, or some other technique you like) to identify possible problems. Continue marking till you have worked all the way through a page or several pages, depending on how many marks you make. Then refer to your handbook to complete the necessary changes. A methodical approach helps you resist the temptation to start taking shortcuts and leave some of the work undone.

Slow yourself down when you proofread. Read aloud to someone else, or read the last paragraph and then the next to last and so forth, working your way back toward the beginning. You have to change your reading technique because, when you read from front to back, picking up speed as you go, you start concentrating on the meaning and overlooking the errors.

Collaborate with peer editors. You don't have to be physically together to read each other's work; you can give your peer editor a copy and talk through it on the phone, or you can send a copy on e-mail. Another pair of eyes can often spot a problem yours missed. When you get your writing back, you can use this book to check your editor's opinions and see how to take the proper corrective measures.

Make it perfect. It is now an hour till the deadline. You have e-mailed your peer editors and the three of you have worked through each other's writing—identifying problems, looking them up, and making the necessary corrections. You look over the pages of your manuscript. They're beautiful, but on page three you see a word repeated, and on page seven you find a question without a question mark. You ask yourself if you couldn't just draw a line through the repeated word and write in the question mark. How many errors can you get away with? You know the answer. If you mark the pages, they won't be beautiful, and everybody expects a printed page to be perfect, without errors or inconsistencies of any kind. With a sigh, you correct and reprint the pages thinking there really are a lot of *Things Your Grammar Never Told You.*

Maurice Scharton
Janice Neuleib

CHAPTER

1

Simple Sentences

Simple pleasures are the last refuge of the complex.

(Oscar Wilde)

This chapter discusses sentences under three headings: Clarity, Variety, and Correctness. Since mastering all the techniques presented here would give new meaning to the phrase *life sentence*, you should know the purpose of each section.

- Clarity focuses on how to give writing readability and force;
- Variety focuses on unusual sentence structures that serve rhetorical purposes;
- Correctness focuses on tidying up errors in sentence construction.

Clarity

Like a skimpy bathing suit, clarity can save a lot of guesswork. When you have something you want your reader to see, you will need to represent your meaning economically, guide your reader to the important points with emphasis, and remove obstacles that impair your reader's sense of flow.

Empty Phrases

The following phrases add to the length of a sentence without increasing its interest or information.

They are the verbal equivalent of warts. You know what to do.

Wordy Phrase	*Replace with . . .*
along the lines of	like, resembling
as a matter of fact	actually [or delete]
aspect	[delete]
at all times	always
at the present time	now
because of the fact that	because
dimension	[delete]
for the purpose of	to, because
in order to	to
it is; there is/are	[delete]
kind of a	[delete]

Wordy	In fact, it is the conscience aspect that hurts when everything else feels so good.
Improved	Conscience hurts when everything else feels good.

COMPUTER TIP

Use the grammar and style checking function of your word-processing program to help you hunt for empty phrases.

- Set the grammar checker for the level of style (e.g., formal, casual, technical) that suits the audience, purpose, and occasion of your work.

Needed Words

Don't get overenthusiastic about cutting "excess" words. If your sentence reads like the instructions on a medicine bottle or the radio chatter in an action movie, you've gone too far. Reread to check for missing words, and add them when necessary.

Words in compound structures

You may omit repeated words in compound structures, but don't lose the reader with fragments or garbled grammar.

Seeing is believing except _{when you're} seeing television commercials.

Without "when you're," you have to read the sentence twice to get the joke. In case you were wondering, adding a comma before *except* would worsen the problem by adding a punctuation error to an already flawed sentence.

A skeptic is someone who is never in doubt about his doubts and _{whom} no one can reassure.

Young writers—how touchingly naive—still trust in _{and} write by grammatical rules.

Without the addition of *in*, the reader will try to use *by* with *trust*. "[T]rust by" is not idiomatic English.

The word *that*

If you drop out the word *that*, check the sentence for ambiguity.

She often feels _{that} her cat's fur is made of silk.

Is she petting the cat or expressing an opinion about the cat? Without the addition of *that*, you may have to read the sentence twice to know.

The one function _{that} TV news performs very well is that when there is no news we give it to you with the same emphasis as if there were. (David Brinkley)

Without the word *that*, a reader might try to figure out which stations offer "one function TV news." The word *that* keeps the noun phrase "[t]he one function" separated from the noun phrase "TV news."

COMPUTER TIP

Use the mouse to move selected text short distances.

- You don't have to cut and paste text that you're only going to move a short distance.
- Just select the text, then point, click, and hold.

- Continue holding the mouse button down and move the mouse to the insertion point.
- Release the button.

Words in comparisons

In complex comparisons, supply words to lead the reader to the comparison you have in mind.

> those of
> No self-respecting cat has claws longer than ∧ dogs.

The comparison isn't clear without the reference to claws. If you happened to be present when the reader looked at your sentence, you could argue that "dogs" is an abbreviated form of "dogs' claws," but you'd need an apostrophe to support your argument. In any case, you'd lose the reader even if you won the argument.

Lively Verbs

If a sentence is just lying there lifelessly, not expressing an action, you can resuscitate it with a new verb. As a rule, replace the following verbs:

- to be
- seems
- have
- make
- go

To Be and *Seems* as Linking Verbs

Lifeless	It *seems to be* unwise to represent one-self in court.
Lively	One should not *represent* oneself in court.
	Lawyers who *represent* themselves have fools for clients.

Note that the verbs of the second and third sentences inject a little adrenaline into the subjects. After you've given the sentence CPR, you can usually put it to work conveying more information, so a third draft of the sentence is often warranted.

HAVE

Lifeless	You *have* the ethical responsibility to bring about a change in the state of the environment.
Lively	You should *help save* the environment. *Give* a hoot; don't *pollute*.

MAKE

Lifeless	Our judgments *were made* on the merits of individual cases.
Lively	We *judged* each case on its merits. No good deed *went unpunished*.

Sometimes thinking through the second draft of a sentence brings to mind a little witticism, which becomes the third draft of the sentence. It is as impolite to refuse these gifts from your unconscious mind as it is vain to hope that you can consciously produce more of them.

GO

Lifeless	The money will *go* to those who make the best arguments.
Lively	The money will *flow* toward the most persuasive people. Better ideas *attract* bigger bucks.

If you focus on revising the verbs listed, you will probably get the idea of lively verbs and perceive that other verbs occasionally need this sort of attention. Act on those perceptions when they occur.

Don't obsess on verbs. The idea is to bring the subject to life, not to do a grammar exercise. Feel free to use *to be* as an auxiliary in a sentence like Dave Barry's:

> If a woman *is forced* to choose between catching a fly ball and saving an infant's life, she will choose to save the infant's life without even considering if there are men on base.

In this sentence, *is,* a form of *to be,* is an auxiliary to *forced,* a lively verb.

Should inspiration strike, feel free to use *to be* as a linking verb to express a wise saying, profound truth, or smart-aleck comment:

> Depression *is* just anger without enthusiasm.

COMPUTER TIP

Use the search function of your word-processing program to look for verb forms that you may want to revise.

- Specify a search for all forms.
- Otherwise, you'll have to run separate searches for *go, went,* and *gone; have, has,* and *had.*

Specific Nouns

Improving clarity can be a simple matter of changing a few nouns.

- Examine the subject of each sentence.
- If the subject contains an abstraction or a generality, consider whether you can replace the abstraction or the generality with a more concrete or specific equivalent.
- Give the sentence one more look to make sure it fits into the context of the piece you are writing.

There are strong differences between my views and the views of mainstream society.

My off-center beliefs distinguish me from the average American.

I think I'm diagonally parked in a parallel universe.

The nouns grow more specific with each revision: different views become off-center beliefs, which give way to the diagonally parked metaphor. Likewise, "mainstream society" becomes "the average American," which transforms itself into "a parallel universe." The second draft of the sentence improves noticeably on the first while the third version provides a little moment of delight, perhaps occasioned when the writer thought to rephrase the square-peg-in-a-round-hole cliché.

Note that sometimes abstract and general language works wonderfully well to convey understated irony.

I regard you with an indifference closely bordering on aversion. (Robert Louis Stevenson)

COMPUTER TIP

Your word-processing program's grammar and style checker may include a calculation of readability, expressed as the grade level required to read your writing.

- While a readability formula can't tell whether you've written well, it can use word and sentence length to estimate the difficulty your language might present a reader.
- Before and after editing for variety, check your writing to see what your changes have done to the readability level.

Flow

When people say that a piece of writing flows, they mean that the writing provides a smooth reading experience. Sometimes flow is compromised by little collisions of words and meaning. With some effort, a reader can usually see what the writer meant, but the reader loses the sense of flow. Think of the problems that follow as splattered bugs on your reader's windshield.

Sexist Language

It is good manners, not political correctness, to give everyone a place in language. Thus the objections to sexist terms such as *mankind, chairman, authoress,* and *actress* no longer require explanation or justification, and the following advice has to do with practice, not with political perspective.

Replace words that specify a single gender where both genders are implied or where specifying gender creates a prejudicial tone.

Sexist	To boldly go where no *man* has gone before . . .
Appropriate	To boldly go where no *one* has gone before . . .
Sexist	One can tell when an *actress* has been too well trained.
Appropriate	One can tell when an actor, such as *Meryl Streep* has been too well trained.

The issue of whether to write *he* or *she* can be resolved by using either plurals or specific examples. It is no more difficult to write, "You can always recognize well-informed people because they share your views," than to write the sexist, "You can always recognize a well-informed man because he shares your views."

COMPUTER TIP

Find sexist language automatically.

- Your word-processing program's grammar and style checker may have a check box for sexist language.
- Start the checker, and then look at the list of options or settings to turn on the feature.

Confusing Shifts

With this set of clarity problems—shifts in grammar and meaning—the affected sentences start out going in one direction and then wander off aimlessly in another, leaving the impression that the writer may have suffered a blow to the head.

Point of view

Point of view (*I, we*—first person; *you*—second person; *he, she, they*—third person) should remain consistent. Observe junior prom etiquette: stay with the person who brought you.

> In ancient Egypt cats were worshipped as gods. This makes *them* [not a *cat* or *him*] too prone to set *themselves* [not *himself* or *herself*] up as critics and censors of the frail and erring human beings whose lot they share. (P. G. Wodehouse)

Since you started with the plural *cats*, you have to keep the pronouns plural all the way to the end of the sentence.

The second person point of view (*you*) works for giving instructions or otherwise directly addressing a reader. But *you* is inappropriate in formal contexts.

> The book's author contends (and *one* hopes he's joking) that *one* should study three hours for each class hour.

Don't shift from *one* to *you* to avoid a tone that's too formal or stiff. You have to stick with *one* once you start. If you're afraid you're starting to sound like the Prince of Wales, rephrase the whole sentence.

> The book's author contends (he must be joking) that a student should study three hours for each class hour.

Shifts in tense, mood, voice, and aspect

Keep readers in touch with the sense of the text by staying with the same tense throughout.

Keeping verbs consistent is sometimes easy.

> The trouble with telling a good joke *is* that it *is* sure to remind someone of a bad one.

The first verb *is* represents present tense, and the second *is* matches it.

> They *get* up so early because they have so much to do and *go* to bed early because they have so little to think about. (Oscar Wilde)

The first verb, *get,* is present tense, so the second verb, *go,* must also be present tense.

The situation grows more complex when the sentence contains a hypothetical case.

> If you *ask* some people how they are, they *will* expect you to listen to the details.

The verbs *ask* and *will expect* represent a hypothetical cause-effect chain beginning in the present and extending to the future. Idiomatic English requires that the first verb be in the present tense and the second verb add the auxiliary *will* to indicate future time.

Very literate people can create a sentence that requires half a dozen grammar rules to sort out.

> If the world *should blow* itself up, the last audible voice *would be* that of an expert saying it *can't be done.* (Peter Ustinov)

A hypothetical condition is expressed in the verbs *should blow* and *would be.* The second set of verbs, *would be* and *can be done,* time-warp you forward to listen to the expert, who is being quoted exactly.

When writing about a literary author or work, it is conventional to use the present tense.

George Bernard Shaw often *criticizes* democracy as a set of false promises, "the last refuge of cheap misgovernment."

When the literary discussion turns from the author and the work, you use past tense where it is appropriate.

Sentimental writing once *caught* the interest of certain Victorian readers who *thought* of themselves as sensitive souls.

Mixed Constructions

The phrase *mixed construction* can be translated as *verbal roadkill*. The reader is zipping along and then suddenly there appears a mangled, flattened creature that may once have been a sentence. You can be pretty sure the reader won't slow down to have a closer look.

Mixed grammar

Writers sometimes change direction abruptly in their thinking or partly revise one sentence and then go on to the next sentence, leaving behind a dizzying sentence and a reader fumbling for Dramamine™.

Avoid shifting from subordinate to coordinate connectors.

When you're in doubt, so mind your own business.

Omit *when* or *so*.

When you're in doubt, mind your own business.

Shifting plans for the sentence

The writer began the following sentence planning to write, "In my favorite story by Flannery O'Connor, a woman gets her wooden leg stolen by a Bible salesman." But halfway through the sentence, the writer decided to add the idea that the story "makes fun of intellectuals," or perhaps the phone rang.

In my favorite story by Flannery O'Connor in which a woman gets her wooden leg stolen by a Bible salesman makes fun of intellectuals.

To edit the sentence, you could remove the word *in,* you could add the word *anti-intellectual* before the word *story* and delete *in which,* or you could write two separate sentences.

> *Just because* we got into this mess stupidly *doesn't mean* we can't get out the same way.

The phrases "Just because" and "doesn't mean" take the sentence in two different directions. You have to decide whether you want to write "That stupidity got us into this mess doesn't mean it will get us out," or "Just because stupidity got us into this mess, I supposed it could also get us out."

Mixing indirect and direct question forms

Indirect questions put subject before verb. Direct questions require an auxiliary verb before the subject.

Indirect   She asked whether she might be excused from further maternal attention.

Direct   "Mother," she inquired, " may I grow up now?"

To write an indirect question, you paraphrase direct question form. If you combine the two forms to create, "She asked could she be excused," a reader will expect you to follow with a Huckleberry Finn sentence, "Me and Tom, we was a-wantin' the Widder to leave us be likewise."

Illogical Connections

Occasionally, you'll find little patches of gibberish that the writer's body wrote while the mind was taking a nap.

Illogical   Better than marrying a millionaire, it's divorcing one.

Logical   If there's one thing better than marrying a millionaire, it's divorcing one.

Illogical   I wonder why it is when people who want eternal life but can't fill an afternoon.

Logical   I wonder why people long for eternal life when they can't fill an afternoon.

Misplaced or Dangling Modifiers

A misplaced modifier sometimes amuses but more often confuses the reader. Be careful to place the modifier near the word or words it modifies. Modifiers should directly modify the noun, verb, or adverb:

Misplaced Modifiers	We *almost* gave away all the beanie babies.
	We *only* have six frenzied shopping days left till Christmas.
	Running down the hill, my nose began to itch.
	Always suspect any job men vacate for women *willingly.*
Correctly Placed Modifiers	We gave away *almost* all the beanie babies.
	We have *only* six frenzied shopping days left till Christmas.
	Running down the hill, I felt my nose begin to itch.
	Always suspect any job men *willingly* vacate for women. (Jill Tweedle)

An awkwardly placed modifier creates a bull-in-a-china-shop impression. The prudent reader is more inclined to scramble out of the way than to read on.

Awkward Placement	Most modern calendars, by reminding us that each day that passes is the anniversary of some perfectly uninteresting event, mar the sweet simplicity of our lives.
Effective Placement	Most modern calendars mar the sweet simplicity of our lives by reminding us that each day that passes is the anniversary of some perfectly uninteresting event. (Oscar Wilde)

Some academic writers habitually prefer awkward placement, perhaps because they confuse difficult reading with sophisticated thinking or because they want to defend themselves against argument. However, the very brightest people often write the kind of ordinary, straightforward prose that invites reading and discussion.

| Awkward Placement | Youth is life untouched by tragedy as yet. |
| Effective Placement | Youth is life as yet untouched by tragedy. (Alfred North Whitehead, *Adventures of Ideas*) |

Split Infinitives

An infinitive consists of the word *to* followed by a verb. To split an infinitive is to put a word between *to* and the verb. Avoiding split infinitives is like crooking your pinky when you hold your teacup.

College is a fountain where some come *to drink,* some to sip, and some *to* just *gargle.*

College is a fountain where some come to drink, some to sip, and some just *to gargle.*

Some writers split infinitives for clarity and rhythm, as in "to boldly go where no one has gone before," and some readers forgive them.

COMPUTER TIP

Shift-click to select an irregular quantity of text.

- Place your cursor at the beginning or end of the section you want to select.
- Then use the scroll bar to move to the other end of the section to be selected.
- Hold down the shift key, point, and click the exact spot.

Variety (A Tiny Style Handbook)

Effective writers vary sentence length and structure to balance the demands of clarity and emphasis. A writer's personal way of managing variety is referred to as the writer's style (or voice). For a reader, a writer's style should fade from conscious awareness, as well-designed patterns of all kinds will—from rock and roll rhythms to Winnie-the-Pooh wallpaper. The style should emerge from the background only to guide a reader to interpret the text accurately and expressively.

Parallelism

An often quoted example of parallelism, expressing comparable ideas in similar grammatical structures, is Henry David Thoreau's advice on how to live a better life: "Simplify, simplify, simplify." A writer could hardly express ideas in a simpler parallel structure than three verbs separated by commas, but then Thoreau was referring to life in a shack near a pond. Writers with more demanding lives use parallelism in less overt ways.

> She is a frank, charming, fresh-hearted young woman who married for love. (Katherine Anne Porter, *The Necessary Enemy*)

This sentence illustrates an elegant use of parallelism. Porter uses three modifiers to list three good qualities the young woman possesses. She then separates a fourth quality ("who married for love") and expresses it differently, in a *who* clause, signaling that she will treat it differently. Porter might have written the sentence "She is a woman who is frank, charming, and freshhearted, and who married for love," but that structure would have read less clearly and emphatically, and it would have seemed to equate dissimilar ideas. In the next sentence, Porter continues and complicates the pattern by repeating *she, young,* and *who.*

> She and her husband are one of those gay, good-looking young pairs who ornament this modern scene rather more in profusion perhaps than ever before in our history.

As she writes the second sentence, she repeats the basic pattern of the first sentence. Her plan goes something like this: list the good qualities, repeat *she,* repeat a form of the verb *to be* and *young,* use the noun pairs in the slot where *woman* occurred, repeat the *who* clause. Porter echoes but does not recreate the parallel series a paragraph later when she uses *she.*

> She is dismayed, horrified, full of guilt and forebodings because she is finding out little by little that she is capable of hating her husband, whom she loves faithfully.

She hints at but ends the parallel series because she is expressing a meaning quite contradictory to her opening. It doesn't matter whether Porter spontaneously created this parallelism or whether she revised to achieve it. What is important is that she has used sentence structure to guide the reader to important comparisons and contrasts.

To create parallel structures at strategic spots, you simply copy the pattern you have established.

- Locate a sentence or two that contain related ideas.
- Revise the second sentence to repeat the pattern of the first.

Sentence Beginnings

Use consistent sentence beginnings to help a reader make sense of a paragraph. The beginning of a sentence usually contains "old" information that is more familiar to the reader than the "new" information nearer the end of the sentence. In long, complex sentences, use consistent phrase and clause beginnings for the same purpose.

In the following three sentences, Dorothy Parker satirically describes an oddly decorated room. References to a ridiculous statue of a boy serve as the old information that hold the three sentences together, allowing her to use extended descriptions to achieve ironic effects in the rest of the sentences. In the third and longest sentence, Parker uses references to chariots and horses in an old-new-old information pattern to organize her description of an awful picture of a chariot race.

> On the heavily carved mantel was a gaily colored figure of a curly-headed peasant boy, ingeniously made so that he sat on the shelf and dangled one leg over. He was in the eternal act of removing a thorn from his chubby foot, his round face realistically wrinkled with the cruel pain. Just above him hung a steel-engraving of a chariot-race, the dust flying, the chariots careening wildly, the drivers ferociously lashing their maddened horses, the horses themselves caught in the moment before their hearts burst and they dropped in the traces. (Dorothy Parker, "The Wonderful Old Gentleman")

Readers rely on the old-new pattern to connect each new sentence to the paragraph as they read it. To keep the pattern consistent, check the beginnings of sentences.

- Look through a paragraph to determine whether old information (introduced in the first sentence of the paragraph) appears in the first part of each sentence.
- If the beginning of a sentence appears to contain unfamiliar information, check to see if the information was introduced near the end of the preceding sentence.
- If you can't find an old connection for new information in the beginning of a sentence, consider filling in another sentence that creates the connection or else deleting or moving the sentence.

Combining Choppy Sentences

If your style is choppy—that is, if you overuse short sentences—your reader will grow bored, or worse, begin to notice the similarity and miss your meaning. Often, choppy sentences can be repaired by a process called embedding, combining in a single sentence the ideas that might be expressed in two or three separate sentences. The following forty-four word sentence illustrates how embedding works.

> I went to the woods because I wished to live deliberately, to front only the essential facts of life, and see if I could not learn what it had to teach, and not, when I came to die, discover that I had not lived.(Henry David Thoreau, *Walden*)

The sentence is not easy to read, but if you respect Thoreau's thinking on complex issues, you stop to wrestle with him. When Thoreau wrote this sentence, he expressed a thought whose muscularity we can appreciate if we divide the sentence into several shorter, wimpier sentences.

> I went to the woods
>
> I wished to live deliberately.
>
> I wished to front only the essential facts of life.
>
> I wanted to see if I could learn what life had to teach.
>
> I did not want to discover, when I came to die, that I had not lived.

By combining this set of ideas into a single sentence, Thoreau presents a complex rhythm of thought in which the ideas seem to battle one another. Notice that the sentence seems to start and then hesitate and then go on again and again. This see-saw effect is achieved by allowing words and word groups to interrupt sentence flow as "when I came to die" does by separating the adverb *not* from the verb *discover.*

In learning to create embedded sentences, you are well advised to start simply.

- Locate a few of your shortest sentences, those that read like "I went to the woods" and "I wished to live deliberately."
- Combine them using a subordinating conjunction (e.g., *after, although, as if, because, before, even though, if, however, since, so that, than, though, unless, until, when, where, whether, while*).
- Use coordinating conjunctions (*and, but, for, nor, or, so, yet*) sparingly because they create a listlike, even juvenile, effect.

COMPUTER TIP

Use average sentence length and readability to diagnose choppy sentences.

- Run the spelling and grammar checker.
- Notice the average sentence length and the average readability levels it reports.
- As a rule of thumb, consider combining sentences that average fewer than ten words in length.

Varying Sentence Structure

You must trade clarity to get emphasis, as a pilot must trade speed to gain altitude. To give your writing rhetorical height, you can use a periodic sentence: one that creates a climactic rhythm by presenting its most important idea last, requiring the reader to hold the rest of the sentence in mind until the final words of the sentence allow a simultaneous release of tension and resolution of the thought. The following periodic sentence, which emphasizes the word *truth,* occurs in the conclusion of Henry David Thoreau's *Walden.*

> Rather than love, than money, than fame, give
> me truth.

Strategically, it makes sense to use periodic sentences in concluding paragraphs to bring a sense of finality and closure to a piece of writing.

Periodic sentences are easy to construct. You simply rephrase the sentence so that the point you want to emphasize comes at the end. If Thoreau's sentence were rewritten

- by Bill Gates, it might read "Rather than love, than truth, than fame, give me money."
- by Madonna, it might read "Rather than truth, than love, than money, give me fame."

If you want to tinker with a periodic sentence to improve its effectiveness, you can work on parallelism (expressing related ideas in similar ways). Thoreau's use of parallelism involved simple repetition of *than* to help build the reader's sense of anticipation about the last item in the series.

Extending Sentences

You can write a long but quite readable sentence by using a pattern called the cumulative sentence. Begin with a simple statement. Then add phrases and clauses that elaborate on the statement.

Henry David Thoreau begins an extended cumulative sentence with "I sometimes dream of a larger and more populous house." He builds his dream house in 341 words.

> I sometimes dream of a larger and more popu-
> lous house, standing in a golden age, of endur-
> ing materials, and without gingerbread work,
> which shall still consist of only one room, a vast,
> rude, substantial primitive hall, without ceiling
> or plastering, with bare rafters and purlins sup-
> porting a sort of lower heaven over one's head,—
> useful to keep off rain and snow, where the
> king and queenposts stand out to receive your
> homage, when you have done reverence to the
> prostrate Saturn of an older dynasty on stepping

over the sill; a cavernous house, wherein you must reach up a torch upon a pole to see the roof, where some may live in the fireplace, some in the recess of a window, and some on settles, some at one end of the hall, some at another, and some aloft on rafters with the spiders, if they choose; a house which you have got into when you have opened the outside door, and the ceremony is over; where the weary traveller may wash, and eat, and converse, and sleep, without further journey; such a shelter as you would be glad to reach in a tempestuous night, containing all the essentials of a house, and nothing for house-keeping; where you can see all the treasures of the house at one view, and everything hangs upon its peg that a man should use; at once kitchen, pantry, parlor, chamber, storehouse, and garret; where you can see so necessary a thing as a barrel or a ladder, so convenient a thing as a cupboard, and hear the pot boil, and pay your respects to the fire that cooks your dinner, and the oven that bakes your bread, and the necessary furniture and utensils are the chief ornaments; where the washing is not put out, nor the fire, nor the mistress, and perhaps you are sometimes requested to move from off the trapdoor, when the cook would descend into the cellar, and so learn whether the ground is solid or hollow beneath you without stamping. (Henry David Thoreau, *Walden*)

Thoreau uses subordinate clauses beginning with *as, if, where, when, wherein,* and *which;* coordinate clauses beginning with *and;* appositives based on *house* and *hall;* and a host of phrases beginning with prepositions and participles. If you disassemble and reassemble this sentence, you will learn virtually everything there is to know about cumulative sentences.

Cumulative sentences can be somewhat complex to punctuate, but they're easy to write—so easy, in fact, that politicians and preachers favor them.

- Start with a simple sentence, one you might ordinarily think about combining with another because it sounds a little weak, a sentence such as "Cumulative sentences are easy to write."

- In your mind, rephrase the sentence as a question (e.g., "Why are cumulative sentences easy to write?" or "How easy?" or "For whom?").
- When you have thought of an answer (e.g., "because cumulative sentences operate by adding phrases and clauses, usually separating the additions with commas"), add the information: "Cumulative sentences are easy to write; so easy, in fact, that politicians and preachers favor them because they operate by adding phrases and clauses, usually separating the additions with commas."

Passive versus Active Voice

In a passive sentence, the action is mentioned before the actor. In an active sentence, the actor is mentioned before the action. Either kind of sentence may contain an object, someone or something that is acted upon. You should change passive sentences to active unless you have a good reason for using a passive structure.

In the following passive sentence, the action is cursing, the actor is the woman, and the object is the library.

> That a famous library has been cursed by a woman is a matter of complete indifference to a famous library. (Virginia Woolf, *A Room of One's Own*)

In this passive sentence, notice that the object, *library,* precedes the action, *cursed,* and that the actor, *woman,* comes last of all in the sentence. Woolf wanted to emphasize the *library,* rather than her action taken against it, so she chose to put the object first. This move de-emphasizes the role of the actor, which is not something writers ordinarily want to do.

In active sentences, actors precede actions, and actions precede objects. Woolf uses the actor-action-object order three times in a later sentence.

> Never will I wake those echoes, never will I ask for that hospitality again, I vowed as I descended the steps in anger.

The sentence reads a little more easily than her first sentence: Woolf places her actor, *I,* before the

actions *wake, ask, vowed,* and *descended.* Her objects—
echoes, hospitality, and *steps*—occur after the actions.

Check to be sure that you use actor-action-object
order unless you have a good reason to put the object first.

- Find the action being performed in a sentence.
- Identify the actor. (You may have to supply an
  actor that is only implied, as in "the library was
  cursed." Who cursed it?)
- Rephrase the sentence to put the actor before
  the action. ("The woman cursed the library.")

COMPUTER TIP

Don't trust the grammar checker.

- If you use grammar and style checking function
  of your word-processing program to locate passive
  constructions, ask a grammar expert to double-
  check the sentences the program identifies.
- The computer sometimes can't tell passive from
  active, nor does it know when you have used
  passive voice effectively.

Correctness

It's best to save this work until you have finished all
the other changes since work to improve clarity or variety sometimes produces problems of correctness. If
any of the errors listed in this section appear in your
papers, you must, for the sake of your teacher's
sunny disposition, keep a list of both the errors and
the sentences containing them. Refer to the list when
you do your last proofreading. Teachers grow cross
and sometimes despondent if these errors continue
to appear.

Subject–Verb Agreement

In theory, subject–verb agreement is as simple as
monogamy, a matter of finding commonalities and
negotiating agreement between individuals that
seem to belong together. In practice, unfortunately,
subject–verb agreement also resembles monogamy.
Anyway, singular subjects require singular verbs,

plural subjects plural verbs. In "I cling to my opinions," the singular subject "I" takes the singular verb, "cling." In "We cling to our opinions," the plural subject "We" takes the plural verb "cling."

Here are the subject–verb patterns:

PRESENT TENSE

I live	We live
You live	You live
He, she, it lives	They live

PAST TENSE

All forms use *lived.*

The verb *to be* works differently from other verbs as it has special forms.

PRESENT TENSE

I am	We are
You are	You are
He, she, it is	They are

PAST TENSE

I was	We were
You were	You were
He, she, it was	They were

Elements inserted between subject and verb

Elements that separate subject and verb may cause confusion when the inserted phrase or clause contains nouns that do not agree with the subject of the verb. Look for the subject of the verb, not the closest noun:

A *number* of different approaches *is* being tried (that's what we tell customers when we have no idea what we are doing).

Communism, like other revealed religions, *is* largely made up of prophecies. (paraphrased from H. L. Mencken)

The prepositional phrase makes the meaning plural, but the grammar remains singular.

If several nouns intervene, the reader awards you extra points for difficulty when you get the verb right:

We shouldn't complain because all this *traffic* on the street—the honking cars, smelly trucks, ugly vans, and weaving motorcycles—*means* that in some far-off paradise there are empty parking spaces.

Compound subjects joined by *and*
These can be confusing, so read the example carefully. The compound subject, which includes *hard work* and *careful moderation*, requires the verb *allow*.

Hard work to advance in one's profession to gain a higher salary *and careful moderation* of expenses to create a sizable inheritance *allow* a parent to protect a child from the disadvantages that gave the parent a strong character.

Stripped of the confusing stuff, the basic proposition is that hard work and careful moderation allow a parent to protect a child from disadvantages.

Tea and sympathy, once the title of a play about a sexual liaison between a young boy and a sympathetic woman, *has* become a catch phrase for inappropriate attention.

The phrase "Tea and sympathy" works as a unit in this sentence.

Compound subjects joined by *nor* or *or*
The verb must agree with the closest subject.

If major policy issues *or* better yet a minor *scandal is* being discussed, the press will fly in lazy circles over any political gathering.

The compound subject includes *issues* and *scandal.* The subject with which the verb must agree is *scandal,* not *issues,* so the verb should be *is:* a minor scandal is being discussed.

Collective nouns
Words such as *couple, group, congregation, class, jury,* and *committee* are considered singular in United States publications.

The *couple is* invited to dinner.

Even if the two members of the couple quite dislike each other, arrive at different times, and leave with different people, the word is still singular.

An exception is made when the individuals within a group are clearly being referred to in the text:

A *couple* who *are* in love for the first time believe that they invented it.

Half the class *were* listening with their mouths instead of their ears.

Collective units of measurement are singular.

Three-fourths of the pizza is gone.

Reversed word order (verb before subject)

Occasionally a writer will put the verb before the subject for variety or emphasis.

At my parents' house *are a family album* full of embarrassing photographs *and a Bible* detailing much history, including all my marriages.

The subject is plural: a family album and a Bible are at my parents' house.

Place holding by *there*

There does not determine the number of the verb following it, since it is not the subject; rather, the subject follows the verb.

There are a *cat and a dog* in my house.

Rephrase: *A cat and a dog are* in my house.

There was *a day and a night* to live through.

Rephrase: *A day and a night were* to be lived through.

By rephrasing, you can see what the proper verb should be.

Singular meaning, plural form

Some words that end in *-s* can be singular.

Statistics is my favorite subject (yeah, right).

Statistics are usually more important than aesthetics when Hollywood decides whether a movie is to be produced.

Words such as *aesthetics, economics,* and *statistics* are singular when they refer to a single subject matter, but plural when they refer to groups of things.

Titles and words as words
A title is singular; so is a word.

J.R.R. Tolkien's *Unfinished Tales* illustrates that myth is not synonymous with falsehood.

Mars, the god of war in Roman mythology, gave his name to words such as *martial,* which means "having to do with war," but not to *martini,* a drink that has occasionally kept men from going to war.

Indefinite pronouns as subject
Although indefinite pronouns (e.g., *anyone, someone, everybody, somebody,* and *everyone*) may seem to be plural, they are considered singular in formal American English.

Nearly *everybody* at the opera *has* a good nap.

Indefinite pronouns can cause some awkwardness in gender politics.

Everyone is entitled to *his or her* opinion on the subject.

Everyone requires the singular pronouns *his* or *her,* though the sense of the word clearly implies more than one person.

Special note on sexist usage   Before the middle of the twentieth century, indefinite pronouns were paired with masculine pronouns when the gender of the person referred to was indefinite or unspecified. Some old-fashioned writers cling to the habit, now considered impolitic, of using *his* in an indefinite way to refer to a group of mixed or uncertain gender. Other more modern and liberal writers, including some deluded handbook authors, advocate "Everyone is entitled to their own opinion," which thoroughly muddles the singular–plural issue. Egocentric writers who think themselves cute prefer "Everyone is entitled to my own opinion," which is no help. The obvious solution, "Everyone is entitled to its own opinion," won't do either, leaving modern writers with a choice between *his or her* and rephrasing the sentence with *we* or some other word that is grammatically plural.

We are entitled to *our* opinions on the subject.

All, any, and *some* may be either singular or plural depending on their referents.

All the *boys have* scout uniforms.

All the *ice cream* is gone.

The boys are individuals, which calls for a plural verb. The ice cream is a mass, which calls for a singular verb. Considered together, the boys, the uniforms, and the ice cream call for a visit to the laundry.

Relative pronouns (*who, which, that*) as subject

Verbs agree with the antecedent of the relative pronoun (see Chapter 6, pp. 165–170, on grammar for detailed definitions).

Lives that require too much self-examination *are* not worth living.

The plural antecedent, *lives,* of the relative pronoun, *that,* requires a plural verb, *are.*

His interest in foreign languages is one of the *things*—his lack of scruples is another—*that help* him get ahead.

The subject of the verb *help* is the pronoun *that.* The antecedent of *that* is *things,* a plural noun. The verb should therefore be plural: *help.* It's easy to be confused by the singular nouns *one* and *interest,* which lead you to expect, until you get to the prepositional phrase "of the things," that the sentence will contain two singular verbs.

Should you just rewrite?
A sentence that is correct but odd will make the reader want to box your ears.

Another thing to consider *are the whips and chains.*

The writer is using inverted word order and referring to the whips and chains as a unit, so she could argue that the sentence is correct, but that's not the sort of argument a busy reader needs. It's easier to edit the sentence to make the agreement clear.

We also want to consider *whether we should furnish the dungeon with whips and chains.*

There, that's better.

Special Problems with Verbs

Irregular verbs
English verbs have regular and irregular forms. (See Verbs, pp. 169–170, in Chapter 6.) Regular verbs form a past tense or past participle simply with *-d* or *-ed,* but irregular verbs change form in a variety of ways. You may need to consult a dictionary if you have doubts about irregular verbs. A simple rule is to use the past tense when there is no helping verb and the past participle when a helping verb appears.

saw (have seen)
We ~~seen~~ many unusual creatures in New York at
the zoo and on Broadway.

Two irregular verbs, *lie* and *lay,* cause an extraordinary amount of confusion and anxiety. If you have trouble keeping them straight, breathe deeply and count to three.

1. Try connecting *lie* and *lay* with *sit* and *set.* You can usually substitute *sit* for *lie* and *set* for *lay.*

   To annoy Mother, I *lie* on the couch and *sit* on the kitchen counter.

   I *lay* the newspaper on the bathroom floor and *set* dirty dishes under the bed.

2. The present participle of *lie* is *lying;* the present participle of *lay* is *laying.*

I am *lying* on the couch in my pajamas.

She is *laying* down the law.

3. The past participle of *lie* is *lay;* the past participle of *lay* is *laid.*

I *lay* there yesterday morning watching *Scooby-Dooby-Do.*

She *laid* the groundwork for an insanity plea.

Now exhale.

Tense

In simplest terms, tense indicates present or past time. Tense shifts, the most common problem writers encounter, are discussed in the Clarity section.

Survey of tenses
(See Verbs, pp. 169–170, in Chapter 6 also.)

PRESENT TENSE

Singular

I	talk, write, am
you	talk, write, are
he/she/it	talks, writes, is

Plural

we	talk, write, are
you	talk, write, are
they	talk, write, are

PAST TENSE

Singular

I	talked, wrote, was
you	talked, wrote, were
he/she/it	talked, wrote, was

Plural

we	talked, wrote, were
you	talked, wrote, were
they	talked, wrote, were

FUTURE TENSE

I, you, he/she/it, we, they	will talk, write, be

The perfect tenses represent more complex time and meaning relationships.

PRESENT PERFECT

| I, you, we, they | have talked, written, been |
| he/she/it | has talked, written, been |

PAST PERFECT

| I, you, he/she/it | had talked, written, been |

FUTURE PERFECT

| I, you, he/she/it | will have talked, written, been |

Each tense also has a progressive form that expresses complex future action.

PRESENT PROGRESSIVE

I	am talking, writing, being
you	are talking, writing, being
he/she/it	is talking, writing, being

PAST PROGRESSIVE

I	was talking, writing, being
you	were talking, writing, being
he/she/it	was talking, writing, being

FUTURE PROGRESSIVE

| I, you, he/she/it, we, they | will be talking, writing, being |

PRESENT PERFECT PROGRESSIVE

| I, you, we, they | have been talking, writing, being |
| he/she/it | has been talking, writing, being |

PAST PERFECT PROGRESSIVE

| I, you, he/she/it | had been talking, writing, being |

FUTURE PERFECT PROGRESSIVE

| I, you, he/she/it | will have been talking, writing, being |

Special uses of the present   The present tense appears when the writer talks about literature or expresses general truths.

> Mr. Henry James *writes* novels as if it were a painful duty. (Oscar Wilde)

> A modern Polonius may *say,* "To thine own subject position be true, and it will follow as the night the day thou canst not then be marginalized in any social episteme."

The past perfect   This verb form is usually combined with a past tense verb to show actions completed in the past.

> We decided to continue the beatings until the
>   had been
> morale ₍∧₎ ~~was~~ improved.

Mood

English verbs have three moods: indicative, used most of the time to express most ideas (I *think;* therefore I *am*); imperative, used to express orders or advice (*don't go* near the water); and subjunctive, used for conditions contrary to fact (if wishes *were* horses, beggars *would* ride). The subjunctive has all but disappeared from English, except in stylized situations.

Present subjunctive uses only the infinitive (see Verbs in Chapter 6, pp. 169–170) of the verb.

> He was so incompetent as a teacher that we insisted he *be* promoted to administration.

Past subjunctive now uses only *were.*

>   were
> If the world ₍∧₎ ~~was~~ fair, celery would give you wrinkles and chocolate would define your abs.

Voice

Voice in transitive verbs (see Chapter 6, p. 175) is classified as active and passive.

Active voice places the actor in the subject position.

> Some *people* make difficulties,

Passive voice places the recipient of the action in the subject position.

> And some *people* are made by difficulties.

Passive   What is learned from history is that
           nothing can be learned from history.

Active   We learn from history that we learn
           nothing from history. (George Bernard
           Shaw)

Casual writing tends to use active voice, whereas
formal academic writing may require passive voice.

Pronoun–Antecedent Agreement

Pronouns (*he, she, it, you, they,* and so on) cause problems of agreement or reference when they are separated from the nouns they represent. They don't
mean to cause trouble; they just seem to get lonely.

The word that a pronoun refers to is called its antecedent. The antecedent defines the number of the
pronoun.

Singular   The *physicist* theorized about the re-
            sults of *her* research.

Plural   The *physicists* argued about the mean-
            ing of *their* research.

Singular   What would women say if a man
            changed the length of his trousers
            every year?

Plural   What would women say if men
            changed the length of their trousers
            every year? (Lady Astor)

When the antecedent is indefinite or collective,
the singular must be used in standard English,
though writers are sometimes tempted to use the
plural (see Subject–Verb Agreement, pp. 24–25).

The community that won't spend ^its ~~their~~ money
on schools this year should save the money to
build prisons in ten years.

Indefinite pronouns

These pronouns refer to nonspecific things. They are
always singular, even when they appear to be plural
(*anybody, anyone, each, either, everybody, everyone, everything, neither, none, no one, someone, something*).

No one who *is* paid by the word can afford to be
careless with ~~their~~ hyphens.

Note that *is,* the verb following *no one,* is singular, which should clue you to change the plural pronoun *their.* In this case it's best to delete *their.* You could also replace *their* with *his or her,* or you could rephrase the sentence using a plural pronoun.

> *Those* who *are* paid by the word must be careful with their hyphens.

Use the pronoun *you* when giving orders; don't use *you* as an indefinite pronoun.

> Take a big step if *you* need to. *One* [not *you*] cannot cross a chasm in two small jumps. (paraphrased from Lloyd George)

The first sentence gives an order and uses *you.* The second makes a generalization that requires the indefinite pronoun, *one.*

Generic nouns
These nouns seem to be plural, but they are referred to as singular.

> *Every* student must bring *his* or *her* [not *their*] ticket.

> An aspiring author must prepare *himself* or *herself* for constant frustration.

Collective nouns
Nouns such as *group, family, couple, committee,* or *team* are considered singular when the group members are referred to as a single unit.

> The Griswold *family* often gave *its* hosts a rough time.

An exception is made when group members are referred to as individuals.

> The Griswold *family* decided that *they* should *all* wear funny hats.

Unclear referents
Readers expect a pronoun to refer to the immediately preceding noun. If more than one noun might be the referent, readers are forced either to reread or go on in confusion.

The referent is the word referred to by the pronoun. The referent is also called an *antecedent* because it goes before something. "*Ante*" is the Latin prefix for "before," and "*cedo*" means "to go."

> *Parents* can always depend on children to quote *them* correctly when *they* have said something *they* shouldn't have.

The sense of the sentence is that when parents say something indiscreet, children repeat the parents' words at an inopportune moment. The pronouns *them* and *they* refer to parents, but, unfortunately, the noun *children* intervenes between the pronouns and *parents*, forcing the reader to struggle with the pronouns. Ideally, you want the reader to think, oh, that was well said, so a little rewriting is in order. The problem occurs in the clause that gives information about the parents beginning "when they have said. . . . " Moving that information closer to the noun *parents* should help.

> Parents *who say something they shouldn't have* can always depend on children to quote them correctly.

The second version is less ambiguous than the first since the noun *parents* now precedes the pronoun *they*. The pronoun *them* is still stranded. Reversing the order of the sentence will help. It's the children who are causing the trouble (both in real life and the sentence).

> Children will always correctly quote *parents* who have said something *they* shouldn't have.

Now, that's well said.

To create emphasis, you may occasionally write a sentence that requires a reader to stop and reread.

> In fairyland, we avoid the word "law"; in science *they* (scientists) are fond of *it* (this word). (G. K. Chesterton)

> Chesterton influenced Lewis in most of *his* (Lewis's) work.

Implied reference
Pronouns may not refer to a noun that isn't there.

Say something you shouldn't have when you want
your ideas
~~them~~ to be quoted exactly.
‸

Without "your ideas," the pronoun *them* would be
pointing to something invisible.

Modifiers may not serve as antecedents.

For Pooh's birthday, *Pooh* [not *he*] wanted a new
balloon.

If you wrote *he* instead of *Pooh,* the only noun your
pronoun could refer to would be *birthday,* which is
nonsense.

Vague referents of *this, that,* or *which*

All relative pronouns (see Chapter 6, pp. 166–168)
must have specific referents.

Vague	*This* is just a little nut that held its ground.
Specific	*This huge oak* is just a little nut that held its ground.

Intensive *it*

Don't use *it* to intensify a noun.

Incorrect	In history, *it* teaches us that men and nations behave wisely once they have exhausted all the other alternatives.
Correct	*History* teaches us that men and nations behave wisely once they have exhausted all the other alternatives. (Abba Eban)

Case of personal pronouns

Pronouns in the subject or subject complement position take the subjective case, and pronouns in object
positions take the objective case. Possessives take the
possessive case.

Subjective	*Objective*	*Possessive*
I	me	my
we	us	our
you	you	your
he/she/it	him/her/it	his/her/its
they	them	their

Most native English speakers use these forms easily, but a few situations involving the choice between *I* and *me, she* and *her, he* and *him,* and the like may cause difficulties.

Compound word groups   Sometimes compounds make your eyes cross for just a minute. Simply remove all but the pronoun to see what should be used.

> In fair weather and foul, he believes that his friends and *he* [not *him*] can see better fifty feet distant from the play than the officials can see from five feet away.

> Please send your complaints to my editor and compliments to *me* [not *I*].

By rephrasing to "he can see" and "send your compliments to me," you can see which pronoun fits.

Subject complements   A subject complement is a noun or pronoun in the predicate that is the same as the subject. Be careful to use subjective case pronouns for subject complements.

> It was *she* [not *her*] who said that as one gets older, the pickings get slimmer, but the people don't.

If the subjective case pronoun sounds too formal, simply rewrite the sentence.

> She said that as one gets older, the pickings get slimmer, but the people don't.

Appositives   Appositives must take the same case as the word or words they rename.

> We poets, Mr. Yeats and *I* [not *me*], disagree about the world of elves; he sees them as anarchists; I see them as hopelessly rule bound.
> (G. K. Chesterton, paraphrased)

> Read "I disagree," not "me disagree."

> Elves probably wouldn't have much to do with either of us, Mr. Yeats or *me* [not *I*].

> Read "to do with me," not "to do with I."

We or *us* before a noun   Choose the pronoun that would work if the noun were not in the sentence.

> *We* [not *us*] modernists may say broadly that free thought is the best of all the safeguards against freedom. (G. K. Chesterton)

Read "we may say."

> Words can mean anything they like to Alice in Wonderland or to *us* [not *we*] postmodernists.

Read "to us."

Pronoun after *than* or *as*   Verbs are often dropped after comparisons using *than* or *as*. Test your choice by finishing the clause.

> He is more in love with himself than *she* [not *her*].

Read "than she is."

> But she is more in love with love than him [not *he*].

Read "than with him."

Pronoun before or after an infinitive   An infinitive is the form of the verb that uses *to* (see Chapter 6, pp. 169–170). Both subjects and objects of infinitives require the objective case.

> Our principles forced John and *me* [not *I*] to ask Sam and *him* [not *he*] to abandon their principles.

Read "principles forced me to ask him."

Pronoun or noun before a gerund   A gerund is a verb form that functions as a noun. Pronouns and nouns before gerunds always take the possessive case.

> Tom's and *my* [not *me*] agreeing on a choice of restaurants led to *his* [not *him*] falsely inferring that I shared his chichi taste for white wine.

Who or *whom*   *Who* is subjective and *whom* is objective. These pronouns appear in subordinate clauses (see Chapter 6, pp. 175–176) or in questions. Substitute *him* or *her* for *whom* to be sure you've chosen correctly.

> *Whomever* [not *whoever*] you like will be chair.

Substitute to make the sentence read, "you like *him* [not *he*]." Since *him* fits, then *whomever* is the right choice. Don't you just love it?

Whom [not *who*] did the Princess kiss in the garden?

Read "the Princess did kiss *him.*"

Whoever is near will do when you aren't near *whomever* you love.

Substitute to make the sentence read, "*she* is closest," and "you love *her.*"

Adverbs and Adjectives

Adjectives modify nouns, and adverbs modify verbs, adjectives, or other adverbs. Adverbs often end in *-ly,* but this rule of thumb doesn't always hold, for some adjectives end in *-ly* (*friendly* cat) and some adverbs don't (*very* hot). See Chapter 6 (pp. 168–171) for more detail.

Adverbs

At times in casual speech or writing, adjectives are substituted for adverbs, but in standard English contexts, only adverbs modify verbs, adjectives, or adverbs.

Adverbs modify verbs, adverbs, or adjectives.

The motel suited the Griswolds just *perfectly* [not *perfect*].

He was *really* [not *real*] sorry he ate the armadillo.

Good often appears for *well* in casual speech and writing, but again, this usage is not recommended.

Tommy did *well* [not *good*] in his parole hearing.

Adjectives

Adjectives are usually placed before nouns, but can follow nouns as complements after linking verbs.

Their hearts are *kind.*

Problems can occur after the verbs *appear, smell, taste, look, feel,* and *grow.* Figure out whether the word describes a noun or a verb to decide whether to use an adjective or adverb.

Adjective	The *horse* looked *curious* when I began to mount on the wrong side.
Adverb	The horse *looked curiously* at me as I picked myself up off the ground.

| Adjective | The frog looked *curious.* |
| Adverb | The frog looked *curiously* at the Princess's pucker. |

Linking verbs are usually followed by an adjective since linking verbs don't express action and therefore aren't modified by adverbs.

He looked *poor* [not *poorly*] after meeting the pickpocket.

I don't feel *good* [not *well*] after eating two hot fudge sundaes, but I'm happy.

Comparatives and superlatives

Adjectives and adverbs have three forms: positive, comparative, and superlative (see Chapter 6, pp. 168–171). One-syllable words add *-er* or *-est.* Two-syllable words vary with usage. Three-syllable words use "more."

sad, sadder, saddest

innocent, more innocent, most innocent

quick, quicker, quickest

swiftly, more swiftly, most swiftly

Some adjectives cannot be compared.

ideal, unique

Use the comparative to compare two things and the superlative for three or more.

I asked her to rent whichever of the two movies had the *greater* [not *greatest*] number of machine guns and explosions.

She returned with the *most* estrogen-enhanced spoons-and-lace extravaganza in the video store.

I am sure she felt her choice was *ideal* [not *the most ideal*], as did I when I awakened from a delightfully refreshing nap.

Which of the two stories has the *sadder* [not *saddest*] ending?

She ran the *most* [not *more*] swiftly of the thoroughbreds in the race.

That choice was the *ideal* [not *most ideal*] one.

Sentence Boundary Errors

For now, when you write in school or business contexts, you must punctuate sentences conventionally.

When you become a poet, novelist, ad writer, or CEO, you can punctuate any way you want to and call it your "style." Until then, creative punctuation counts as an error.

Fragments

Sentence fragments contain a phrase or dependent clause beginning with a capital and ending with a period. Generally, conventional punctuation requires that phrases (subjects without verbs or verbs without subjects) or clauses with subordinating words (*because, that, which, since, if,* etc.) be connected to independent clauses. Connect fragments to adjoining sentences or rewrite them to add the missing element.

Editing the subordinate clause by connecting it to the previous sentence

Fragment	We all have photographic memories. Although we don't all have film.
Revision	Although we all have photographic memories, we don't all have film.

Editing the subordinate clause by constructing a new sentence

Fragment	We all have photographic memories. Although we don't all have film.
Revision	We all have photographic memories. Unfortunately, we don't all have film.

Editing a fragment by connecting it to the appropriate sentence

Fragment	We all have photographic memories. But don't all have film.
Revision	We all have photographic memories but don't all have film.

Editing a fragment by making a new sentence

Fragment	We all have photographic memories. But don't all have film.
Revision	We all have photographic memories. Sad to say, we don't all have film.

Note: Often you can use a colon or an em-dash to mend a fragment that is a phrase.

Fragment	I plan on living forever. So far, so good.
Revision	I plan on living forever—so far, so good.

Appropriate fragments? Educated readers sometimes don't mind sentence fragments that provide emphasis or clarity in the text, but the writer has to have enough authority to make the reader confident that the fragment is deliberate. College degrees, publications, age, money, and other badges of social authority (except, perhaps, for height and good looks) entitle a writer to use fragments. If you lack social credentials, you'd better clear fragments with the next person in the chain of command—your teacher; editor; boss; mother; or your roommate, the English major.

Comma splices and run-on sentences

In a comma splice, independent clauses are joined with a comma rather than with a period and a capital letter, or with a conjunction, colon, or semicolon. In a run-on or fused sentence, the clauses are joined with no punctuation at all. The following examples illustrate editing techniques for comma splices and fused sentences.

Editing with a period and capital letter

Fused Sentence	There are two tragedies in life. One is to lose your heart's desire the other is to gain it.
Comma Splice	There are two tragedies in life. One is to lose your heart's desire, the other is to gain it.
Revision	There are two tragedies in life. One is to lose your heart's desire. The other is to gain it.

George Bernard Shaw, the author of the third set of sentences, must have known that the two separate sentences would make the ideas clear and distinct.

Editing with a comma and coordinating conjunction

Comma Splice	There are two tragedies in life. One is to lose your heart's desire, the other is to gain it.
Revision	There are two tragedies in life. One is to lose your heart's desire, *but* the other is to gain it.
Fused Sentence	Love is grand divorce is a hundred grand.
Revision	Love is grand, *but* divorce is a hundred grand.
Comma Splice	I am in shape, round is a shape.
Revision	I am in shape, *for* round is a shape.

The coordinating conjunction shows that the ideas in the clauses are logically related to each other.

Here's an important safety tip. Don't use a conjunctive adverb such as *moreover* or *since,* or you'll recreate the error you're trying to correct. Your only choices are *and, but, for, nor, or, so,* or *yet.*

Editing with a colon

Comma Splice	There are two tragedies in life, one is to lose your heart's desire, and the other is to gain it.
Revision	There are two tragedies in life: one is to lose your heart's desire, and the other is to gain it.

The colon suggests that the second sentence explains the first.

Fused Sentence	Love is grand divorce is a hundred grand.
Revision	Love is grand: divorce is a hundred grand.
Comma Splice	I am in shape, round is a shape.
Revision	I am in shape: round is a shape.

The colon emphasizes the comment-and-rebuttal relationship between the two clauses.

Editing with a semicolon

Comma Splice	There are two tragedies in life: one is to lose your heart's desire, coincidentally, the other is to gain it.
Revision	There are two tragedies in life: one is to lose your heart's desire; the other is to gain it.

The semicolon emphasizes the close parallelism of the sentences. Even when a movable conjunctive adverb such as *coincidentally* appears in the sentence, the semicolon is still necessary. Subordinating conjunctions (e.g., *since* and *because*) do not require a semicolon and cannot be moved around in the sentence.

Editing with a subordinating conjunction

Fused Sentence	There are two tragedies in life: one is to lose your heart's desire the other is to gain it.
Revision	There are two tragedies in life: one is to lose your heart's desire *while* the other is to gain it.
Comma Splice	Love is grand, divorce is a hundred grand.
Revision	Love is grand *whereas* divorce is a hundred grand.
Comma Splice	I am in shape, round is a shape.
Revision	I am in shape *because* round is a shape.

Note that you don't use a comma before a subordinating conjunction.

Acceptable comma splices?   Not only are there acceptable comma splices, there are even famous ones such as Julius Caesar's; "I came, I saw, I conquered." Short independent clauses in a series, as in the preceding example, usually take commas. Note that the clauses are strictly parallel, word for word and idea for idea. If you want to try to write a snazzy splice, use Caesar's as a model.

Special Problems of English as a Second Language

If you are not a native speaker of English, you may find this section useful as you work to understand and follow our curious linguistic customs. We who grew up speaking English don't claim that it's logical or orderly, but we have grown fond of its quaintness and its quirks.

Articles

The indefinite articles *a* and *an* and the definite article *the* indicate that a noun is about to appear.

Use *a* or *an* before a count noun.

a hamburger

an orange

Note that *a* precedes consonants whereas *an* precedes vowels.

a ranch

an orphan

Do not use *a* or *an* before a noncount noun (an entity that cannot be counted or a personal name).

I like *coffee* but not *tea*.

Noncount nouns include:

Food and drink: coffee, tea, ice cream

Nonfood substances: ice, coal, iron, oxygen

Abstract nouns: fear, attention, energy, joy

Other units or names: chemistry (and all subject names), work, baggage, clothes, lumber, mail, cash, money, prose, poetry

Use *the* when the specific identity of the noun is known because

1. the unit has been identified previously
   A horse ran into the field and stopped suddenly. *The* horse had noticed us immediately.
2. a word group follows and restricts the identity
   Avoid *the* patch of poison ivy at all costs.

3. the context clarifies the noun

> Leave *the* books where you found them.

Do not use *the* with plural or noncount nouns whose meaning is clearly "all" or "in general."

> *Noodles* provide a base for many meals.

> *Spaghetti* also is the center of many a meal.

Helping and Main Verbs

Check your use of helping (auxiliary) verbs with main verbs against the patterns in this section.

Always put helping verbs before main verbs.

> Folks *will* like cold tea in summer.

> *Do* not cross the street.

Have, do, and *be* change form to indicate tenses.

Forms of *do: do, does, did*

Forms of *have: have, has, had*

Forms of *be: be, am, is, are, was, were, being, been*

Modals, verbs of permission, possibility, or emphasis, do not change form to indicate tenses.

> Modals: *can, could, may, might, must, shall, should, will, would* (also *ought to*)

All verbs but one have five forms (*be* has eight). Listed below are the forms for *live* (a regular verb) and *sing* (an irregular verb).

Base form	live, sing
-s form	lives, sings
Past tense	lived, sang
Past participle	lived, sung
Present participle	living, singing

Modal and base form
After modals, use only the base form.

> She *could bake* bread if she wished.

> Artists *should sell* their work to museums.

Do, does, or did and base form
Use only the base form of the verb after forms of *do.*

Bear *does not* often *think* about his future.

Do you *plan* to carry all those packages?

Have, has, or had and past participle

Future, present, and past perfect verbs use *have, has,* or *had* followed by a past participle.

The student *will have passed* the test when she *has written* the last question.

We *had planned* to go to Chicago this weekend, but the rain *has changed* our plans.

Form of be and present participle

To express an action in progress or a planned action, use *am, is, are, was, were, be,* or *been* followed by a present participle.

We *are planning* to eat Chinese food in Chicago this weekend.

I *was riding* my horse last weekend.

Note that the helping verbs *be* and *been* must have other helping verbs before them (see Progressive forms, p. 29).

She *must have been* the only one left.

Verbs showing mental activity are not expressed in progressive aspect in English. Examples include *appear, believe, have, hear, know, like, need see, seem, taste, smell, think, understand, want, wish.*

I *wish* I might go to Grandma's for the holiday.
[Not ever: I *am wishing* I might go.]

Form of be and past participle

To form the passive voice of a verb, use a form of *be* followed by a past participle (see Passive voice, pp. 20–21).

The order *was given* by an unknown general.

All the presents *had been sent* before early December.

In the passive voice, *be* must follow a modal.

The children *would be allowed* in with parents but not alone.

Being follows *am, is, are, was,* or *were:*

I *am being asked* to do double work.

Some verbs (*occur, happen, sleep, die,* and *fall*) may appear to be passive, but they cannot be since they are intransitive. They cannot be given passive constructions in English. [Never: It *had been happened* that. . . .]

Omitted Subjects, Expletives, or Verbs

If the written form of your first language idiomatically omits subjects, expletives, or verbs, check your writing to be sure you haven't carried the habit over into English. Written English omits few words, most notably the subject *you* in imperative sentences such as "[*you*] Think before you act." In the explanations below, the bracketed words must be written out.

[*I*] own my own home.

All the fans came to the game. [*They*] wanted to see the star.

If the subject moves from its regular position, English substitutes an expletive.

[*There*] is only one price for this car.

Verbs may never be omitted in standard English as is possible in some languages.

The price of lobster in Chicago [*is*] very high.

Idioms

Of course all languages have idioms, words and phrases with special meanings beyond denotation (simple dictionary meaning). English idioms often have pictures attached to them: "raining cats and dogs," "ten miles as the crow flies," "has me over a barrel." As with all idioms, each idiom has to be explained to a new user of English.

Repeated Subjects or Objects

In some languages subjects or objects reappear in a clause. This double subject or object form is never allowed in standard English.

My father the violinist ~~he~~ came to America.

Adjective clauses (which modify nouns) never include an object in English, even if the relative pronoun is omitted.

All the visitors crowded into the elevator that was going up ~~it~~.

CHAPTER 2

A Few Words About Words

> The difference between the almost right word and the right word is really a large matter—'tis the difference between the lightning and the lightning bug.
>
> (Mark Twain, *The Art of Authorship*)

Twain is absolutely correct, but like most great writers, he's no help at all. There are hundreds of thousands of words in the English vocabulary, and any one of them may have several meanings and fit into an infinite number of contexts. How can an ordinary mortal writer find the right word when the almost-right word has such a distressing habit of coming to mind first and crowding the right word out? To narrow the scope of the problem, you can learn how meaning develops and how usage changes.

How Words Make Meaning

Like the space–time continuum, a word's meaning can be viewed in four dimensions: denotation, the word's explicit meaning; connotation, its implicit overtones, subtleties, and associations; context, the word's relationship to the message in which it occurs; and etymology, the characteristics of a word that are particular to certain times and places. Consider the word *rose*, for example.

- *denotation:* a fragrant flower with soft petals and sharp thorns
- *connotations:* beauty, romance, love, transience

- *contexts:* gardening manual, a poem, a florist's advertisement, a tattoo parlor's price list
- *etymology:* according to the *Oxford English Dictionary,* the word *rose* entered English near the end of the ninth century A.D. By the end of the tenth century, *rose* was being used in figurative senses of something beautiful yet thorny. Its use as the name of a color can be traced as far back as the early 1500s.

Robert Burns, the eighteenth-century poet who wrote "My love is like a red, red rose" meant for us to understand something different from the gardener who thinks of roses as something you spray for those little bugs called aphids; Burns created a context of rhyme and meter and used a little of the rose's denotative value (" . . . that's newly sprung in June"), but he mainly exploited its connotative associations ("As fair art thou my bonnie lass, / so deep in love am I"). The poem was written in Scottish dialect of the eighteenth century and is often read aloud in that dialect. All of these factors combine to give the word *rose* a meaning unique to Burns's poem.

The four dimensions of meaning can be important, individually or collectively, to reasoning about a word choice. As an editor, you might choose to change *infer* to *imply* because you can tell from the context that the writer means "hint," not "deduce." Or you might change *housewife* to *caregiver* in your own writing because you know about the history of sexist terms and you want to avoid annoying your readers.

How Usage Changes Meaning

One more important factor complicates word choice. Writers always have to ask whether their words create the right impression on the reader. "Do I seem educated?" "Does this sound okay?" "Is this right?" Correct usage is the equivalent of dressing properly for the occasion. Historically, middle-class Americans have believed that learning correct English would lead to social and professional success. (Many of these same people also believed in Santa Claus and the Easter Bunny early in life.) In fact, people who believe in the magical power of correct English have it backwards: it is success that defines correct English, not correct English that promises success. "Correct" English is the language of the most powerful people.

George Campbell (*The Philosophy of Rhetoric,* 1776) explains that correct usage is

- *reputable:* demonstrated by educated and well regarded writers;
- *national:* understood and accepted by the whole country; and
- *present:* not old-fashioned, or foreign, or trendy.

Social Idiom

Idioms are ways of speaking and writing that seem arbitrary, often because their origin has been lost in the history of the language. The common definition of idiom involves colorful phrases such as "fork in the road." The word *idiom* also has a broad meaning: the speaking and writing habits that characterize the people of a region, or class, or profession, or artistic persuasion. Thus we speak of the rap music idiom or the legal idiom or the academic idiom. Someone from a rural background may write in colorful metaphors: "He was tall enough to go hunting geese with a rake." Someone from a military family may write in a version of Army drill instructor talk: "The work will be accomplished ASAP." The idiom of the most powerful people in any group is considered the "correct" form; people use the language of the powerful as a standard to distinguish insiders from outsiders. We can speak generally of "Standard English" only as long as we remember that the standard varies. No single form of English is "correct" for all writing and speaking to all audiences in all circumstances.

So who says we can't use double negatives (not never) or double superlatives (most best)? If "It's me" sounds better, why is it correct to write "It is I"? Why can't we write *alright* if we can write *altogether* and *already*? We can't because writers of Standard English reject ideas expressed in any idiom but their own. If we break the rules for speaking or writing in a particular idiom, we are instantly recognized as outsiders. If we want to become insiders, we must learn the idiom. Certain words or phrases correctly used send powerful signals that we belong to the inside group. If you'd like to test your knowledge of insider usage, take the "Little Usage Test" in Appendix 2, p. 181.

COMPUTER TIP

Find the settings for your grammar and style checker.

- There will be many options, probably in check boxes, for screening individual text features such as jargon and clichés.
- Check all the boxes to be sure that you consider everything.

Word Pairs

Problems with word choice often occur when writers confuse words that have similar meanings, sounds, or spellings. For example, many writers confuse *anxious,* which denotes unpleasant nervous anticipation, with *eager,* which denotes pleasurable anticipation. "I'm anxious to see you" might be interpreted as "I'd rather not see you." These and other dangerous pairs (as usage expert Wilson Follett called them) are explained in the Glossary of Usage on pages 59–70.

Sometimes a writer tries to use elevated language to prove how educated he or she is. Elevated language, like elevator music, just puts most people to sleep, but occasionally a writer will wake the reader to laughter with embarrassing errors. A student trying to think of an impressive synonym for *hypothetical* once wrote that she was making a *suppository* statement. Her instructor resisted the impulse to invent a clever comment and smiled as he wrote in the margin of her paper that yes, hypothesizing and supposing were denotatively related, and yes, there was a word, *supposititious,* that meant something like hypothetical, but she really needed to check out new words in the dictionary before using them.

Errors like the "suppository" statement are called malapropisms, in honor of a silly, pompous lady in Richard Brinsley Sheridan's play *The Rivals,* who commits these errors over and over. The character, named Mrs. Malaprop, advises one character to forget another. She means to say "obliterate him," but she says,

"Illiterate him, I say, quite from your memory."
(*The Rivals*, Act I, sc. ii)

The word *illiterate* does come to mind when some-one misuses a word so outrageously. We forgive students who are trying to improve their language skills. We just laugh at bores who are trying to impress us. If you keep suppository statements and Mrs. Malaprop in mind, eventually you'll develop a healthy (or is it healthful?) skepticism about your memory and the examples you see in print. You may also develop a healthy reliance on your dictionary.

Changes in Meaning, Form, or Function

So long as people use a language, it will change. The inevitable changes in the way we use words cause some trouble for readers and writers, who must decide whether they agree with each change. Certain people seem to like all change, which suggests strongly that they have no taste. Others dislike all change, which suggests the same thing. Among people who have thought about language enough to have an opinion, some will explain, "I saw it in the newspaper" or "Everyone says it" to justify a new word or phrase. For other people, the change must appear in an authoritative source—a dictionary or the speech or writing of some prominent person. For a few people, the change must demonstrably improve the language.

Nonce words

New words coined just for convenience, sometimes called nonce words, always irritate conscientious students of English. One particularly irksome technique involves the use of the suffixes *-ize* and *-wise* to invent questionable words from acceptable ones. Take the word *profit*, which no one would object to, add *-wise* to it, and you have invented a word that, to sensitive readers, looks like the aftermath of unsuccessful surgery. Adding *-ize* to *incentive* achieves the same disagreeable effect. You can also create a nonce word if you shorten an acceptable word such as *obligation* by dropping *-ion* and adding *-e*. This kind of shortening, called back-formation, occurs because the writer doesn't bother to check the dictionary, which would supply the lovely word *oblige*.

Words that shift meaning

While you are learning to take care about coining words, you may as well learn to notice when a word shifts from one meaning or function to another. These subtle changes are maddening to some sensitive readers. Take the meaning of a word such as *housewife*, for example. Some women feel that the term denigrates women, implying that they are married to the house: the word has acquired enough negative connotations to require that writers take care in using *housewife*. The word *homemaker* is used as a positive, or at least neutral, replacement at present, but it sounds a little evasive or possibly patronizing. In any case, the history of English demonstrates that finding another word won't solve the problem permanently. The word *hussy*, now a word with negative connotations of sexual promiscuity, was once a neutral abbreviated form of the archaic word *huswife*. If *homemaker* follows the pattern of *housewife* and *hussy*, it will eventually acquire enough unpleasant associations to require a replacement. Writers just have to keep up with the politics of language.

Sometimes confusion about a word's denotation occurs when people use the word in a more general sense than its original meaning warrants. Generalized use can stretch a word's meaning until it sags like an old sweatshirt, comfortably covering more and more, revealing less and less, and doing its job in a particularly unattractive way. *Meaningful,* as in the phrases "meaningful dialogue" or "meaningful relationship," exemplifies the stretched-out-of-shape word that covers everything and means nothing. Many economics writers seem to believe that *burgeon* means "to grow" when in fact it means "to bud." As far as some political writers are concerned, the verb *decimate* means "to reduce drastically." *Decimate,* which is related to the word *decimal*, means "to eliminate one in ten." Some usage handbooks advise that it is safe to follow the examples set by print media or by the majority of writers; others argue that writers must exercise great care in choosing models to emulate. We count ourselves among the latter group.

Words that shift function

Occasionally, a word will undergo an almost invisible shift in function. For example, the adjective *collectible* is sometimes used as if it were a noun meaning "things that people like to collect." In newspaper ads for garage sales and estate auctions, the word is even given a plural form (*collectible* + *-s*). The nouns *contact* and *loan* are used as if they were verbs meaning, respectively, "to communicate with" and "to lend money." Sensitive readers notice these little shifts and mentally knock a couple of points off a writer's score. You will have to learn to watch for these changes if you want the most careful readers, people who love the language and clear writing, to approve of you. Even if you take pleasure in annoying such people, you have to know what you're doing in order to tease them.

Current changes

The most current changes are often debated (and usually deplored) in the press by usage experts such as John Simon and William Safire. When you get tired of reading serious commentary, you can enjoy humorist Dave Barry, who writes about "Mr. Language Person," a confident but confused grammarian who is patterned after everyone's worst English teacher. Changes that are somewhat older, but still the subject of controversy on grounds of newfangledness, are usually discussed in recent usage handbooks. A usage handbook resembles a dictionary in that it is an alphabetically ordered list of words, but differs from a dictionary in that it cites only words about which some usage debate exists. The usage handbook discusses words in detail and offers advice about using them. The *Merriam-Webster Dictionary of Usage,* an excellent usage handbook, can often resolve these issues. Another often-used resource is Fowler's *Modern English Usage.* Very conservative writers satisfy themselves with the opinion that "If it isn't in Fowler, it isn't allowed."

Inappropriate Tones

A writer's tone (the attitude or emotion implied by the writer's word choice) lets a reader feel the writer's personality or the human dimension of the writer's subject. Like people, a tone can be delightful, confusing, boring, or annoying to a reader. To edit for tone, you really need to consult a rhetorician (an expert in the effects of word choice on a reader); neither a book nor a computer program can help. If you don't know a rhetorician, use several of your friends or acquaintances. Get them to read your work. Their reactions will tell you as much as a rhetorician can, since a rhetorician's knowledge is based on observing how people react to messages.

Euphemism
A writer who paraphrases an unpleasant truth is said to use euphemism, substitution of inoffensive terms for unpleasant meanings. "These characterizations of the nature of the situation are inconsistent with the facts as I understand them" is a euphemistic way to say, "You're a damned liar." Depending on the potential reader and situation, euphemism may make the writer appear authoritative, tactful, pompous, clueless, or fainthearted.

Vogue words
Vogue words and phrases work reasonably well in oral language, so long as the user keeps up to date. But in writing, the vogue phrase of five years ago dates a writer in a way that often interferes with a reader's attention to the message. To write nineties computer-nerd slang such "I'm all about gibs with this phat GPU and DDR SDRAM" alienates people who are not insiders. If alienation is not your intention, write, "I get great blood-and-guts effects in my video games because my video card has a lot of memory."

Jargon
One person's professional communication is another's jargon. A grammarian might write that "BEV speakers routinely eschew copulatives in utterances such as 'He ready.'" In the cartoon strip *Dilbert*, the author of the jargon would hope readers were thinking, "Ooo, how sexy! I love it when you talk jargon to me." In real life, most readers skim over such language and may be annoyed by it. As prosaic as jargon seems, readers usually prefer, "Speakers of Black English usually drop the verb *is* from a sentence such as, 'He is ready.'"

Clichés
Once, a figure of speech such as "as the crow flies" said "aerial cross-country distance measure" as nothing else could. But figures of speech lose luster with

time, becoming clichés, expressions that have become too predictable. You can try to renovate a clichéd figure of speech ("It's a hundred miles across the Mojave desert *as the crow fries*"), but it's usually neither successful nor worth the trouble. Just translate clichés into ordinary language.

Pomposity and pretension

Though most wordiness can be resolved with the techniques of sentence revision for public audiences, some issues of wordiness are related to tone, especially to the tone of the pompous writer who draws out a phrase. You can see how to edit further for wordiness by noting the main content words in a sentence. Take the preceding sentence as an example. The underlining in the example below designates the most important words in the sentence, the words that convey the actual content.

> Though most <u>wordiness</u> can be <u>resolved</u> with the techniques of <u>sentence revision</u> for <u>public audiences</u>, some issues of <u>wordiness</u> are related to <u>tone</u>, especially to the tone of the <u>pompous</u> writer who <u>draws out a phrase</u>. (36 words)

By concentrating on the underlined words, we can see that the sentence is carrying a lot of extra freight. Words such as *techniques* and *issues* don't add much, nor do repeated words such as *tone*. Now that we see the important words, we can use them to rewrite the sentence.

> After a writer reduces wordiness by revising sentences for public audiences, he or she can focus on the drawn-out phrases that signal a pompous tone. (25 words)

We've reduced the sentence length by almost a third. Most sentences carry extra words or phrases that a writer uses unconsciously. Whittling away the extra words sharpens the point of the sentence.

Errors in level of formality

An overly formal or a too casual tone works like choosing the wrong clothes for the occasion—like a white tuxedo at an office party or a bikini at an embassy's afternoon pool party. Everyone recognizes that there are formal and informal occasions for writing. When we sense that the occasion is formal, we try to find formal words.

To understand formal tone, consider the following quotation from the highly formal occasion of John Kennedy's inaugural speech: "Let every nation know, whether it *wishes us well or ill,* that we shall pay any price, bear any burden, meet any hardship, support any friend, oppose any foe to assure the survival and the success of liberty."

Could we improve the sentence if we replaced the words "wishes us well or ill" with "loves us or hates us"? While the meanings of wishing us well and loving us are closely related, the term "loves" is too personal to describe the relationships between nations, and the same is true of wishing ill and hating. In fact, a closer paraphrase of "wishes us well or ill" would be something like "hopes that we will succeed or longs for us to fail." No one level of style or formality suits every situation. The reader or place of publication will dictate the best choice.

What about this sentence?

The university president clearly had a *fabulous* time at the conference.

Fabulous makes the president sound like a fashion designer ("Darling, the brocades are simply fabulous this season").

What is wrong with the level of formality in this sentence?

The football player *stated* that he liked his game.

Stated is too formal for the sentence and the speaker; *said* would be a better choice.

COMPUTER TIP

Use the thesaurus to jog your memory or balance your style.

- When you aren't satisfied with a word choice, select the word and start the thesaurus. If you are coming up entirely blank on a word, type in a synonym or antonym, and let the thesaurus help you. If you are trying to create a similar or contrasting pair of words (e. g., "help and [synonym]" or "worry or (antonym"), the thesaurus may help you to find just the shade of meaning that you need ("help and support" or "worry or amuse").

Glossary of Usage

Certain picky readers treat the way you use the words and phrases in this glossary as a test of your writing ability. You know how those test scores follow you around, so you'll save yourself a lot of grief if you learn to be conscious of the picky distinctions exemplified below. Use the labels (Subtle Idioms, Dangerous Pairs, Tricky Changes, Distracting Tones) to refer to explanations of the picky reasoning behind the usage.

- Subtle Idioms [I]
- Dangerous Pairs [P]
- Tricky Changes [C]
- Distracting Tones [T]

COMPUTER TIP

Double-click on a word to select it.

- Don't struggle to move your mouse slowly across the word. Double-click it instead. You'll get to go to lunch sooner.

---

a lot [I]   Two words, not one.

accept, except [P]   If you tend to spell words the way you pronounce them, and if you pronounce *accept* with an accent from the urban East of the United States, you may misspell *accept* as *except.* The verb *to except* means "to leave out."

adopted, adoptive [P]   The baby is *adopted;* the parents are *adoptive.* Ideally, they are all pleased with the arrangement.

adverse, averse [P]   Circumstances can be *adverse,* meaning they are unfavorable. A similar word, *averse,* is applied to people who are in an unfavorable frame of mind with respect to something.

advice, advise [P]   Two ways of annoying people are to *advise* (verb) them or to give them *advice* (noun). In polite company, a professional nuisance is called an advisor.

affect, effect [P]   The verb *affect* means "influence"; the noun means "emotion." The verb *effect* means "bring about"; the noun means "the result of a cause."

affect, impact [C]   An *impact* had better make a crater. Use *affect* for contexts in which *influence* would work.

afflict, inflict [P]   Undesirable relatives *inflict* themselves on you at Christmas if they just show up; if you invited them, you have *afflicted* yourself.

African American, black [C]   It is good manners to keep up with the terms that refer to social groups of all kinds. At this writing, *African American* is the preferred term for Americans of African ancestry. Some members of this group may still prefer *black* or *Negro*. The older terms persist in the names of organizations that have been in existence for some time, such as the United Negro College Fund and the National Association for the Advancement of Colored People.

aggravate, annoy [C]   Everyone knows what *annoy* means. *Aggravate* means something different, "to worsen." You *aggravate* an injury if you bump it or let it get infected.

all ready, already [P]   The one-word version is an adverb ("*already* there"). The two-word phrase means either "prepared" ("I'm *all ready*") or "gathered and waiting" ("We are *all ready* to go").

all right [I]   English provides us with *almost, already, altogether,* and *although.* We even have *albeit.* So if logic prevailed, we ought to be able to drop the second *-l* in *all right.* But logic doesn't happen to prevail with this phrase, which consists of two words. Never mind what you see in rock-and-roll lyrics. The kids are *all right.*

all together, altogether [P]   The first means "gathered"; the second means "entirely." So when your friends are *all together,* you are *altogether* welcome to start the party.

allude [C]   This word is not an all-purpose snazzy synonym for refer. It has the narrow meaning of an "implicit or indirect reference to a text." If you mention the text specifically, you have referred, not alluded, to the text. You usually *allude* to a poem or a speech, not to a conversation or a meeting.

ambiguous, ambivalent [P]   Both words refer to a kind of complexity. The first denotes a text or situation you can read more than one way, as when you find your best friend sending secret notes to your significant other. The second denotes the mixed feelings you have about both of them afterward. We hope they're planning a surprise party.

among, between [I]   If the group includes at least you and two others, you are *among* friends. If you are gossiping with only one person, you are keeping it "just *between* us."

and, or [T]   Don't put these two words together with a slash mark or a hyphen unless you want to sound like a military manual or an IRS document.

anxious, eager [P]   If you experience anxiety, then you are *anxious;* if you experience pleasurable anticipation, then you are *eager.* You're eager to finish a test, anxious about the results.

appendix, appendices [I]   It's classy to use the idiomatic Latin plural, *appendices,* for this borrowed word.

awful, terrible [C]   These words once had distinct meanings that were obvious. *Awful* meant full of awe. *Terrible* meant terror-inspiring. The words have been stretched to cover a range of meanings vaguely negative in nature. *Awesome,* once a synonym for *awful,* is stretching itself to cover a host of positive meanings. You will do the right thing by resisting these regrettable changes.

beauty, glamour [P]   *Beauty* appears when you remove ornament; *glamour* results when you apply ornament.

belie, betray [C]   Creative writers describing people who are trying to conceal something may mistake *belie,* which means "to show a lie," for *be-*

tray, which means "to give away a secret." Write "His angry tone of voice belied his kind words," or "His tone of voice betrayed his anger."

believe, feel [C]   The word *feel* applies to your sixth sense (intuitive feelings), your emotions (hurt feelings), and your stomach and skin (nauseated feeling or smooth feeling): that is quite enough for one word to mean. Use *believe* when you make reference to your opinions, and try to think things through before you believe.

besides, in addition to [T]   Why use three words when one will convey the same meaning without also conveying the tone of a slightly pompous school principal?

between you and me [I]   If you feel like using *I* rather than *me* in this phrase, you are about to hypercorrect (overanxiously change correct to incorrect usage). Someone told you not to use *me* in some other context, and you developed a phobia of the word. Learn not to hypercorrect, or you'll sound like middle management.

blatant, flagrant [I]   A *blatant* error is obvious; a *flagrant* error is outrageous.

broke, bust [T]   When paired with *go,* both of these words convey the notion of losing all one's money, though *bust* does so with a slightly humorous tone. You may use *bust* to mean "break" only if you're writing a novel about the American West.

burgeon [P]   This is a newspaper writers' word that means "to bud," as in "The trees burgeon in the spring." Journalists think *burgeon* means something like "grow at a fast and accelerating rate," and they love to use it to describe the economy or the population. It's amusing, if a little cruel, to correct them.

callous, callus [P]   The first word describes an uncaring manner, as in "a callous reporter interviewing the survivors of a disaster." The second denotes the tough skin on your hand.

can, may [P]   A host of teachers has told you to use *can* in contexts of physical ability and *may* in contexts of asking and giving permission. Nothing has changed here.

cite, site [P]   *Cite* means "mention or refer to," as in "Works Cited." *Site* means "a place," as in "a building site."

clandestine, secret [C]   Use *clandestine* to describe sneakiness, as in "a clandestine visit to the refrigerator at midnight," as opposed to a merely private matter, "a secret wish."

collectible [T]   This adjective (note the *-ible* ending) is used in advertisements as if it were a noun meaning "odds and ends, knickknacks, and the like." You can tell people think it's a noun because they add an *-s* to make it plural. These items are sold at stores with names like "Gifts and Things." To understand why you should not use this word or frequent these stores, look up the word *kitsch* in an unabridged dictionary.

compose, comprise [P]   If you mean "include," use *comprise* ("The list comprises three people"). If you mean "make up," use *compose* ("The party is composed of people from different backgrounds"). You can use these two verbs to convey the same meaning if you are careful about the prepositions. Write "The list is composed of three people," or "The list comprises three people." Just be careful not to use *of* with *comprise*.

consists in, consists of [I]   The secret of good coffee *consists in* filtering the water and grinding the beans moments before brewing. Coffee *consists of* tiny particles suspended in heated liquid.

crescendo, peak [C]   Noise rises in a *crescendo*, to a *peak*.

data, datum [I]   Treat *data* as a plural count noun, like *facts*. Write "These data are." For singular senses, write "This datum is."

decimate, annihilate [P]   Note that the Latin root, *deci-*, is the same as in *decimal*, a system of numbers based on ten. *Decimate* means to "reduce by ten percent"; it refers to the bloody practice of slaughtering one captured soldier in ten. That's bad, but not as bad as *annihilating*, that is, wiping out everyone.

delusion, illusion [P]   Medical conditions such as schizophrenia produce *delusions* such as voices that only the affected person can hear.

Illusions, the everyday fantasies we all carry around, aren't usually treated medically for the simple reason that we would be less sane, not more, without them.

dissatisfied, unsatisfied [I] The prefixes *dis-* and *un-* change the meaning of *satisfied* in different ways. To be *dissatisfied* is to find fault with, as in "dissatisfied with the contract they offered"; to be *unsatisfied* is to feel unfulfilled, usually in some physical sense, as in "the soda crackers left my hunger unsatisfied."

doubtful, dubious [P] These are not synonyms. *Dubious* means "questionable," as in "the dubious honor of becoming a human sacrifice." *Doubtful* means "full of doubt."

each other, one another [P] Two people speak to *each other;* three or more speak to *one another.*

easily, easy [I] We use *easily* only as an adverb ("handled it easily"). *Easy* is used as both adjective ("easy test") and adverb ("Take it easy.")

elder, eldest [P] The *elder* of two, the *eldest* of three.

emigrate, immigrate [P] *Emigrate* from a country; *immigrate* to a country.

emotion [C] Some people think that this noun can be shortened into a verb by dropping *-ion* and adding *-e.* These people would shorten *orientation* and *recreation* the same way. Don't trust them. They are more interested in getting things done than in doing things right.

end, terminate [T] If you choose *terminate* when you mean *end,* you will share consciousness with the "suits" who write letters firing people and canceling insurance policies. This is very bad karma.

enjoy, experience [C] Even if you're not having fun, you can *enjoy* (that is, *experience*) a two-year tenure as president of the school board.

enjoyable, fun [C] *Fun* is a noun, as far as fussy editors are concerned, and not to be used in slots where an adjective such as *enjoyable* would fit. Have *fun,* or have an *enjoyable* time, whichever you prefer, but don't use *fun* in the slot where *enjoyable* fits.

envy, jealousy [P] You feel *envy* about something you desire but don't possess, such as a new car parked in your neighbor's driveway. You feel *jealousy* about something you possess that you fear you may lose, such as your spouse who is sitting on your neighbor's lap. Both of these unpleasant and unbecoming emotions should cause you to reflect on your own attitudes.

exceedingly, excessively [P] Occasionally, you will see someone use *excessively*, which means "overly" as if it were a synonym for *exceedingly*, which means "very."

exception of, to [I] These pesky prepositions give everyone pause—make an exception *to* the rule, make an exception *of* a case.

fatal, fateful [C] If fate is involved, use *fateful*. If death is involved, write *fatal*.

finalize [C] Adding *-ize* to the adjective *final* creates the verb *finalize*. If people could only learn to stop there, perhaps no one would object. But *finalize* leads to *maximize*, which leads to *prioritize*, which leads to the appalling practice of making up a new ugly verb whenever the opportunity presents itself. Where will it all end?

flak, flack [P] The first is anti-aircraft fire and, metaphorically, any kind of criticism or resistance. The second is a press agent.

flaunt, flout [P] *Flaunt* means "show off" (*flaunt* one's jewelry). *Flout* means "arrogantly transgress against" (*flout* the law).

graduated [C] A person is *graduated*—that is, granted a change in educational status—by his or her college. You write, "I *was graduated* with a B.A. in 1997."

head over heels, heels over head [I] You wouldn't ever misuse this phrase, but it illustrates the irrationality of idioms. Think about it. *Head over heels* describes a normal posture. If you say that a person is "head over heels in love," which is about the only way you'll use this phrase, you mean that a person's life has been turned upside down. You should really write "heels over head," but that will have your reader creating mental images of people tumbling off stepladders or engaging in gymnastic sexual practices.

healthy, healthful [P]   Use *healthy* to mean "possessing good health." Your gerbil is healthy if you feed it and clean its cage. Use *healthful* to mean "tending to promote good health." Carrots, broccoli, a good night's sleep, and regular visits to the dentist are healthful. Healthfulness and fun seem inimical.

hopefully [I]   In the following sentence, the word *probably* is a sentence modifier, limiting the meaning of the whole sentence. "Probably, the best man will win." Avoid using *hopefully* as a sentence modifier if you want to seem knowledgeable about the finer points of usage.

housewife, homemaker [C]   The first word may seem unflattering; the second, a euphemism. Either word may be labeled "sexist," since both refer to a poorly paid job held almost exclusively by women. Actually, it is the social practice of undervaluing traditionally female occupations, not the language, that is sexist. You should keep up with the terms that are currently polite usage.

increase, hike [T]   Words such as *hike* (meaning "increase") appear in headlines, where they help the newspaper editor to fit the news into the space. Used in other contexts, headline words create the impression that the writer is a press agent, advertising writer, or ninny.

infer, imply [P]   For "conclude or deduce," use *infer.* For "hint or suggest," use *imply.*

ink [T]   As a verb, *ink* is favored by sportswriters, who use the term to mean "sign" usually a contract. The term can also mean "to stain with ink," but most readers will think of sports first.

in line, on line [I]   In the American Midwest, people stand *in line;* in the East, people stand *on line.* Since the (very influential) network television anchorpersons speak midwestern dialect, most people probably use *in.*

its, it's [I]   *Its* is a possessive pronoun like *his* and *hers.* None of the possessive pronouns uses an apostrophe. *It's* is a contraction of the clause "*it* *is."* Since *Its'* exists nowhere in printed English *it's* no wonder that it has been known to cause *its* users to be ejected from class.

jargon [T] This term refers to annoying in-group language used to address outsiders (e.g., *meaningful dialogue* for "conversation"; *intertextuality* for "references to other texts"; and *interface* for "cooperate"). If you've ever been with people who shifted from English to some other language in the middle of a conversation, you'll understand how jargon affects the reader: you wonder what they're saying, and you fear they may be hiding something.

kicked off, started [T] Football metaphors such as *kicked off* annoy many people, including the greater part of at least one whole gender. Keep that in mind when writing the advertisements for your fund drive. Just write *started*.

lay, lie [P] This one may be hard for you to take. When you write a note saying that you're going to sunbathe, it should read, "I'm going to *lie* out in the sun." *Lay* is used when a grammatical object is involved, as in "*lay* the book down."

less, minus [T] To impart a repellent mathematical tone to ordinary speech, use *minus* where *less* would do ("*less* the cost of the postage").

like [I] *Like* is the Volkswagen Beetle of American English usage. Several generations have used it, often equally innocent of its past uses and enamored of its countercultural mystique. In the eighties and nineties, *like* was a verb meaning "said" and a clause meaning "I thought but didn't say." "He's like, you're late more than I am, and I'm like, whatever." In the sixties and seventies, *like* was a meaningless monosyllable, used to fill pauses—"umm." "That was, like, so cool." In the forties and fifties, *like* identified its user as either a beatnik ("He like plays a like way-out set of bongos") or as a person who didn't know the rule that *as*, not *like*, was the correct choice for dependent clauses: "After three espressos, I feel *as if* [not *like*] I could arm-wrestle Superman and win." Only this last distinction matters to writers of Standard English, who, as a matter of principle, remain unaware of *like*'s other uses.

loan, lend [P]   For spots where a noun is required, use *loan*. For verb spots, use *lend*.

lunch, luncheon [T]   *Luncheon* costs more than *lunch* and usually involves sitting up straight and using your silverware properly.

media, medium [I]   The singular form of *media* is *medium*. The newspapers and television are *media;* television alone is a *medium*.

mixed metaphor [I]   There is a logic in figures of speech that you must attend to or risk producing cartoons or muddles in your reader's mind. Think about what happens in the reader's imagination if you write "take the bull by the horns and look the situation in the eye." Do you want your reader pausing to visualize someone holding onto a bull's horns and staring romantically into the bull's eyes? How about "kick off the campaign for safer streets"? The sentence has football ("kickoff") and war ("campaign") as metaphors for a program intended to reduce violence, not a very consistent message.

more perfect, better [I]   If it's perfect, it can't get better. If it has any imperfections at all, it's not perfect. So more perfect is illogical, despite the fact that Thomas Jefferson wrote "form a more perfect Union" into the American Constitution. Write *better or worse*.

mortician, undertaker [T]   Neither of these terms is evasive enough for some people, which is why we also have *funeral director.*

myself [T]   Certain business writers who fear using *me* incorrectly try to use *myself* in locutions such as "This is important to *myself* and my associates." Use *me* unless you want to sound like the dialogue in a 1940s gangster movie.

orally, verbally [P]   A spoken message is delivered *orally.* A message that is in language, either spoken or written, is delivered *verbally.*

point in time, time [T]   Certain phrases have an unpleasant political odor about them. *Point in time* smells like the Nixon administration. Write *time*.

practical, practicable [C]   *Practicable* means "feasible," as in "a practicable plan," meaning a plan that can be carried out. *Practical* means "useful," as in "a practical guide to computers," one that you can use.

reason is because [I]   Replace *because* with *that,* or, better yet, dump the whole phrase, which tells a reader almost nothing.

regardless [I]   Certain writers believe that adding *ir-* to this word increases its forcefulness. While that may be true, it is also true that using the prefix decreases the perceived literacy of the writer.

some time, sometime [P]   Deleting the space changes the noun phrase ("I need *some time* to get my thoughts together.") to an adverb ("Let's get together *sometime*."). *Sometime* is also used as an adjective that means "former, at some time in the past" ("the *sometime* newspaper editor").

swam, swum [I]   The simple past is *swam* ("The beaver *swam*."). *Swum* is the participle, an irregular verb, one that does not form the participle with *-ed* ("The beaver had *swum*.").

there, their, they're [I]   *There* is a place or place holder (expletive). *Their* serves as a possessive pronoun. *They're* is a contraction of "they are." *They're* likely to be late to *their* own party if they keep sitting *there*.

to, too, two [I]   *To* is a preposition to *show direction* or to function as a part of an infinitive. *Too* is an adverb indicating intensity. *Two* is an adjective showing number. That is probably *two too* many *to* keep straight.

use, utilize [T]   Honestly, there is no good reason to choose *utilize*. The denotations of *use* and *utilize* are virtually identical. *Use* is briefer and less pompous.

verbal [C]   Use *verbal* when you mean "expressed in language, either oral or written." Don't use it as a synonym for *oral* or an antonym for *written*.

whether [I]   You don't generally need to add "or not." The "or not" is often implicit.

which, that [I]   Use *which* with clauses that add a bit of information ("My left hand, *which has a small mole*, is the stronger.") Use *that* with clauses that identify one of two or more possible choices ("the hand that is stronger"). Note that the *which* clause is enclosed in commas.

who, whom [I]   Use *who* where you would use *I* or *he* or *she*. Use *whom* where you would use *me* or *him* or *her.* You often have to rephrase the sentence to figure out which word to use because both these pronouns are routinely shifted away from the object position. In "I wonder _____ she will name," the pronoun is the direct object of name (she will name *me, him,* or *her*). The correct usage is "I wonder *whom* she will name."

COMPUTER TIP

To speed your online work, you can refer to online dictionaries for information about the meaning and, in some cases, the usage of a word.

- Dictionary.com (www.dictionary.com/) and Allwords.com (www.allwords.com/) are both based on the third edition of *the American Heritage dictionary*. They offer usage advice, but you should always cross-check usage advice with more than one source.

- The *Encarta World English Dictionary* (dictionary .msn.com/) also offers definitions and usage advice.

- Even after you cross-check, don't believe everything you read in a dictionary. Remember that usage is a matter of context, and dictionary editors don't know what context you're writing for. Be especially distrustful of advice that any usage is always right or always wrong.

CHAPTER 3

Punctuation Lite

Punctuation is a modern art. The ancients were entirely unacquainted with the use of our commas, colons, & c.

(Lindley Murray, *English Grammar*)

This chapter discusses punctuation. Within each section, the explanations are divided into subsections for situations in which the punctuation is Required or Not Allowed.

Don't Guess! Look It Up!

We have a name for people who punctuate by guesswork and intuition: the name is "poet." Everyone else, including off-duty poets, must look up the rules and use them. Essay writers must give up their little poetic fantasies about punctuating by feel and learn to punctuate by grammar.

Intuitive Fantasy

Some punctuation is optional!

Practical Reality

Wrong! But thanks for playing, and we have lovely parting gifts for you! The correct answer is "Cheesy pastel-

Intuitive Fantasy	*Practical Reality*
	colored plastic report covers are optional." For consistency's sake, you must *act as if punctuation marks were either required or not allowed.*
Just put the punctuation mark where you would pause.	That's backwards. When you read aloud, you may pause, if you want to, where you see punctuation. But you mustn't punctuate to show where you ran out of breath. *Punctuate to set off sentence elements.*
You can use punctuation to make your sentence clearer.	And you can also use spices to disguise the taste of spoiled hamburger, but you should wonder whether it's a good idea. If punctuation seems to clarify a sentence, *consider revising the sentence.*
I'm pretty sure my high school teacher said to punctuate this way. Or maybe I saw it in *Details*.	Uh-huh. Let's follow half-remembered instructions or invent new rules based on questionable models. That's a well-known habit of highly successful people. No sense bothering to *look up the rule or example.*

It's so simple! You don't have to guess about punctuation. You can look it up.

- Find the applicable rule or example.
- Compare your sentence to the italicized portion of the example.
- If necessary, refer to the full explanation.
- Punctuate your sentence and double-check it against the example.

Commas

Commas Are Required

Following the first independent clause (one which can stand by itself) in a compound sentence

> *The early bird gets the worm,* but the second mouse gets the cheese.

The comma and coordinating conjunction *but* function as a period and capital letter would, showing that elements preceding and following the connection could have been punctuated as two sentences. Balanced clauses like these look elegant and sound true. Here's an important safety tip: be sure to use a coordinating conjunction in sentences like this, or you will commit a sentence structure error (see comma splice, pp. 40–42).

Following introductory dependent clauses, those which define other clauses and phrases

> *If Barbie is so popular,* why do you have to buy her friends?

A comma following an introductory clause (or phrase) signals the beginning of the main clause of the sentence.

- The first clause gets the comma because it "depends" on the second clause to complete the sentence grammar. *If,* a subordinating conjunction, creates the grammatical dependency.
- You wouldn't need a comma if you paraphrased the sentence so that the subordinate clause or phrase moved to the end of the sentence.

Why do you need to buy friends for Barbie *if she's so popular?*

Separating items in a series

> Four be the things I am wiser to know:
> *Idleness, sorrow, a friend, and a foe.*
> (Dorothy Parker, *Enough Rope*)

Some handbooks say that the final comma in the series is "optional," because the conjunction *and* replaces the comma. But commas separate while conjunctions connect, so it is illogical to use one to replace the other.

- In law, the series divides at the commas. Thus, if an inheritance is left to Tom, Dick, and Harry, it is split three ways. If it is left to Tom, Dick and Harry, it is split two ways. Both Dick's and Harry's lawyers would insist on the comma before the conjunction in the series.
- A comma before the conjunction will alleviate reader confusion and dismay in lists with long, complex items.

The art department decided to place foundation funds in three categories: financing of special events such as student exhibits, support for ongoing museum presentations, *and* stipends for individual artists' projects based on grant applications.

Though you can punctuate this sentence, don't deceive yourself that you have improved its readability. You would be wiser to rewrite such lumbering constructions (see Clarity, pp. 1–7).

Separating coordinate adjectives

We wanted to buy a *new, tidy, compact, serviceable* house but settled for running the vacuum and washing the dishes.

Coordinate adjectives modify the noun in similar ways and seem equivalent in importance. To test whether an adjective series is coordinate, try joining the adjectives with a coordinating conjunction:

We wanted to buy

a *new*

and *tidy*

and *compact*

and *serviceable* house.

Since each adjective contributes an independent, distinct quality to the noun, adding *and* doesn't sound odd.

Contrast this with the more interdependent series of cumulative adjectives in "We bought a large rambling crowded Victorian mansion."

Revising the cumulative series to "a large and rambling and crowded and Victorian mansion" would sound odd because the adjectives relate to one another as well as to the noun. *Large* and *rambling* both specify qualities of *Victorian,* while *crowded* fights with the other three adjectives a little. Think of cumulative adjectives as siblings, who like togetherness, and coordinate adjectives as only children, who need their space.

With nonrestrictive phrases and clauses

To punctuate these word groups correctly, you must decide whether the information contained in them is nonrestrictive or restrictive. *Nonrestrictive* means "adding extra information." *Restrictive* means "indicating which one among many." Since these are a little tricky (in the same way that Mount Everest is a little steep), you may need to test your example against the two example sentences provided for each subcategory. If you are still confused, refer to the discussion of clauses in Grammar (pp. 175–176).

Adjective clauses (dependent element with subject and verb, functioning as an adjective in a sentence)

> The check, *which should have been here Tuesday,* [nonrestrictive] should solve all our problems, though your suggestion that we knock over a convenience store [restrictive] is not without merit.

"Okay, now here you got your *which* clauses, you got your *that* clauses, and you got your *who* clauses." Oops, sorry. That was the voice of Mr. Hilgendorf, the junior-high football coach who, poor guy, taught seventh-grade history in Greybull, Wyoming, and who once tried to teach punctuation. Try to ignore the voice of your personal Mr. Hilgendorf as you contemplate the teensy, yet crucial differences between nonrestrictive and restrictive clauses.

- The *which* clause modifies *check* and is enclosed in commas because it is nonrestrictive.
- Contrast the *which* clause with the *that* clause, "that we knock over a convenience store." The

that clause identifies the particular suggestion discussed. Always use *which* for nonrestrictive clauses and *that* for restrictive clauses.

Who clauses work like *which* clauses:

- None are more taken in by flattery than the proud, who wish to be first and are not. (Benedict de Spinoza, *Ethics*)
- That is, the *who* clause is separated from the rest of the sentence with a comma because it adds a piece of explanatory information.

Adjective phrases

Nonrestrictive	Televangelists, *overdressed and overbearing*, are the pro wrestlers of religion.
Restrictive	Televangelists *on cable at night* help me get to sleep.

The nonrestrictive adjective phrase adds a bit of information:

- Can be moved (to the beginning of the sentence, for example) without further rewording the sentence.
- And is set off with commas to indicate that it is not intended to restrict the statement to a particular televangelist.
- If we drop "overdressed and overbearing" and replace it with the phrase "on cable at night," which does restrict the statement to a certain group of televangelists, the resultant sentence is written without commas.

Appositive phrases (renaming the noun)

Nonrestrictive	We hoped to be taken up into the aliens' mother ship on New Year's Day, *the first day of the new millennium.*
Restrictive	We were huddled with friends on a mountaintop in Montana waiting for the aliens to land on New Year's Day *2000.*

The italicized phrase in the first example offers a piece of information that modifies *Day;* on the other hand, the year *2000* identifies a particular New Year's celebration, requiring no commas. Consider this your invitation to the party.

With sentence interrupters

Sentence interrupters (such as parenthetical expressions) require the reader—poor overworked person that he or she is—to pause, one hopes for a good reason, to process some afterthought that has occurred to the writer before, finally, reaching the sentence's end.

Transitional expressions

> *On the other hand,* we may just get together for a New Year's Day brunch and slip a little something extra into the orange juice.

Expressions such as "on the other hand," "moreover," "therefore," and "thus" seem brief, so you may be tempted to think of the comma that accompanies them as optional. It's better to have a good reason either to use or not to use a comma. In this case, keep in mind that these phrases modify the whole sentence, and the comma helps to emphasize the importance of the phrase.

You might move "On the other hand" to the middle of the sentence. You would then put commas on both sides. If you moved it to the end of the sentence, you would use a single comma. But don't do that: it would sound lame.

Parenthetical expressions

> The speed of life in the fast lane, *my favorite life path,* may have voided the warranty on my body.

Parenthetical expressions slow the flow of reading and thought, so use them only when you want to focus the reader on the information in the sentence. The parenthetical information should truly clarify or add necessary emphasis to the sentence. If you seem to need parentheses frequently, ask yourself why you're wandering off the main subject of the sentence. If you're not careful, you'll end up in graduate school in English, writing term papers with huge digressive footnotes and sentences that read as if they were translated from German.

Absolute phrases

> *The human race being what it is,* I find it hard to be a humanist.

Like many other elements you set off with commas, the absolute phrase is movable. If you moved it after *hard,* you would put commas at the beginning and end of the phrase. You might also use dashes to set off the absolute phrase more emphatically.

The absolute phrase is grammatically interesting because it resembles a clause but isn't one: like a clause it has a subject, but the absolute phrase has a "verbal" instead of a verb. If you didn't get an A in grammar all the way through school, you should probably cross-check this kind of phrase with dangling modifiers. If you think it is at all possible to punctuate this phrase with a semicolon or a period, you absolutely must seek professional help: make an appointment with your family grammarian.

With personal titles, addresses, and dates

> Janice Neuleib, Ph.D.

> Send the renewal form to Janice Neuleib, *Writing Program Director,* 4240 English Department, Illinois State University, Normal, IL 61790–4240.

> The passport will expire on *June 12, 2009,* unless I renew it sooner.

> My birthday was listed incorrectly as 11 June 1943.

Within direct address, short answers to questions, tag questions, quotations

Direct address

> "Is it true, *Professor Einstein,* that the theory of relativity first occurred to you as you contemplated how time spent with one's relatives seems to pass so slowly?"

Short answers to questions

> "*Yes,* that's true."

Tag questions

> "I gather you won't be attending Thanksgiving dinner then, *will you?*"

Quotations

> "*No*," he replied. "I will be working on a unified field theory that first occurred to me as I observed the marching band lining up on the yard markers at the Rose Bowl."

For certain special F/X

Punctuating correctly all the time licenses you to experiment occasionally in the interest of achieving a particular and premeditated effect. Don't try to become the George Lucas of punctuation, but now and again you may use a comma to

- replace omitted words, as in "Offering is little; *giving, much*";
- separate deliberately repeated words, as in "Whatever *will be, will be*";
- structure unusual phrasing, as in "Authors who *can, write* for hours."

Commas Are Not Allowed

Separating compound elements that are not independent clauses

> Bears hibernate in the *winter and* wake up grouchy in early spring.

Does this sentence need a comma after *winter*? No. The sentence has a compound verb, *hibernate . . . and . . . wake,* but it does not have two independent clauses. You would use a comma if the sentence read "Bears hibernate in the winter, and they wake up grouchy in early spring." Adding a second subject, *they,* connected with the second verb, *wake,* creates two independent clauses. For further details, look up Clauses (pp. 175–176) in the Grammar section, but make sure your answering machine is working. You'll be busy all afternoon with the most important and complex concept in grammar.

Between subjects and verbs or between verbs and objects

> Before beginning an argument, *you should* ask *yourself whether* the person you are addressing is a fool or a knave.

How about a comma after *you* or one after *yourself* to indicate a dramatic pause for effect, like that used by the announcer on *Saturday Night Live*? Absolutely not. How about a colon after *yourself*? Nope. If you have a list following a verb, skip to the discussion of colons to learn what to do. In general, don't imitate the punctuation habits of people who wear headsets while they work.

Before or after a series

We *present the* king, the queen, and the *knave* as today's players.

You've put a comma after *king* and another after *queen,* even though someone told you the second one was optional. You're in a comma mood. Should you throw in a comma after *knave* and maybe one after *present* for good measure? In a word, huh-uh. If you think about where you got the idea for that sort of punctuation, you'll probably remember a page filled with pictures of supermodels in their underwear.

Separating cumulative adjectives, adverbs and adjectives, or an adjective and the noun it modifies

In the *crumbling old stone mansion* lives a *ferociously angry troll* with crazed, mysterious eyes.

All these descriptive words—*crumbling, old, stone, ferociously, angry*—and commas already separate *crazed* and *mysterious.* Surely a comma wouldn't hurt somewhere else, would it?

Actually, yes, a comma would hurt.

- The first set of modifiers is cumulative, meaning that they work together as a unit to modify *mansion.* Try reading the sentence as "In the crumbling and old and stone mansion. ..." Adding *and* helps you to see that separating the adjectives is not a good idea.
- The second set of modifiers includes another closely related unit: an adverb, *ferociously,* that modifies an adjective, *angry.* Together they modify the *troll,* noun that he is.

- Don't even think about putting a comma between *mysterious* and *eyes*.

After a coordinating conjunction (*and, but, for, or, nor, yet, so*)

We entered, *but we* soon left because the party felt like a spacewalk—cold and airless.

Does it seem that you could use a comma after *but*? If you replaced but with *however,* you would need a comma, but then the rest of the punctuation would change because *however* is a conjunctive adverb, not a coordinating conjunction. "We entered. However, we soon left because it was clear we were not welcome." Learn to use sentence grammar (coordinating conjunction vs. conjunctive adverb), not sentence meaning (*but* vs. *however*), to punctuate. You'll feel better about yourself, and it's much cheaper than therapy.

Before an indirect quotation

H. L. Mencken *said that conscience* is the inner voice that warns us somebody may be looking.

Directly quoted, the sarcastic comment from Mencken would be rendered as, "Conscience is the inner voice that warns us somebody may be looking." When you drop the quotes, you also drop the comma and the ceremony of direct quotation; your tone becomes ironic and knowing. Don't pretend you thought up the witticism; a graceful citation of the source is cool (see Citations, pp. 151–160, for direction on how to handle the reference).

After *such as* or *like*

It's easier to be nice to him if you think of him as an animal *such as a* wolverine.

People often get two or three punctuation patterns run together in their minds. If you believe a comma might go between *as* and *a* in this sentence, check Colons (p. 87) and Transitional and Parenthetical expressions (p. 77), where you'll probably find the pattern you're remembering. And don't generalize this case—no comma required after *such as* or *like*—to include other similar words. Punctuation is a matter of specific cases, not general rules.

With a question mark or an exclamation point

"Let's do it!" was Gary Gilmore's final advice to the Utah firing squad that shot him.

A comma after an exclamation point? Oh, please! You never use a comma after end punctuation. Period.

Before a parenthesis

For my birthday, just give me your *presence* (*unless,* of course, you would prefer to give me your absence).

Commas before parentheses fall under the heading of "Punctuation Errors Found in Stone-Age Cave Drawings Created by People Who Were Eaten by Saber-Tooth Tigers Before They Could Reproduce." Why people still commit these errors baffles scientists.

Semicolons

Semicolons Are Required

Connecting closely related independent clauses

Thoreau said, "*I came to the woods to live deliberately*"; as for me, *I came to the woods because my parents dragged me screaming and struggling into the station wagon.*

The two clauses make a point about the same subject—going to the woods—which suggests to the writer that clarity might be served by joining the clauses with a semicolon. The writer could also have written them as two separate sentences. To keep from over using the sentence structure of two clauses connected with a semicolon, save these constructions to emphasize one or two important points in a paragraph. Since the resultant sentence can easily run twice the length of your usual sentences, use parallel language (e.g., the repetition of "I came to the woods") to help readers negotiate the greater distance from capital letter to period.

With a conjunctive adverb (*however, moreover, consequently*) or other transitional phrase connecting independent clauses

Invisible means "transparent" or "too small to be seen"; *consequently,* a glass has something in common with a germ.

Words and phrases such as *consequently* have no effect on the need for a semicolon between independent clauses.

- Drop *consequently,* and you still need a semicolon.
- Use a comma instead of a semicolon before *consequently* in this context, and you will commit an error called a comma splice. Only coordinating conjunctions (*and, but, for, nor, or, so, yet*) authorize a comma as punctuation when the conjunction begins the second of a pair of independent clauses.

Separating items in a series with internal punctuation

To keep from going to sleep when your significant other makes you attend the symphony, listen first to the *horns, woodwinds, and flutes*; then the *violins, violas, and cellos*; and finally the *timpani, chimes, and the piano.*

It's hard to read this sentence because it contains a list of lists: the writer is grouping the instruments into wind, string, and percussion sections. Commas wouldn't help you navigate here; you'd get lost somewhere in the oboes and never find your way back to your seat. Since you know that each list ends at the semicolon, you can "chunk" the information in your mind before going on to the next list. You can imagine from reading this sentence that the writer must have a good reason for its difficult construction: she is describing a process and keeping the parts of the process together.

Semicolons Are Not Allowed

After a dependent clause

> *However much you want to win the contest,* you must
> practice to achieve your goal (unless, of course,
> you decide to cheat).

You can't use a semicolon here because the clause
beginning with *however* is dependent; you can only
use semicolons to connect independent clauses.
"However much you want to win the contest" is a dependent clause because it begins with a subordinating conjunction.

However can serve as either a subordinating conjunction or a conjunctive adverb. In this case, it is
used as a subordinating conjunction, meaning "no
matter how" ("No matter how much you want to
win . . . . "). When you use *however* to mean "nonetheless" or "at any rate," it is a conjunctive adverb.

After an introductory phrase

> *In that event,* you may actually win.

Don't use a semicolon just because you're bored
with commas. Take a break or get a snack; come back
to proofreading when you're ready to be serious.
And don't get the idea that semicolons are dressed-
up commas. You need a pair of independent clauses
or a list with internal commas to justify a semicolon.

Between independent clauses joined with a coordinating conjunction

> *The wedding was to be the party of the century, so I*
> *threw caution to the winds and bought a five-hundred-*
> *dollar dress;* the father of the groom can't afford
> to look dowdy.

Together, a comma and coordinating conjunction
serve the same function—connecting independent
clauses—as a semicolon. So you're overdoing punctuation if you use a semicolon with *and, but, for, nor,*
so, and *yet.*

Special explanation for engineers   If punctuation
were arithmetic, a semicolon and coordinating
conjunction would be 1.5 times more punctuation

than you would need for a pair of independent clauses.

Before a list

Kindergarten teachers, the Marines of public education, are the "first to fight" and must prepare for anything, so they study *in a variety of areas:* early child development, language acquisition, and psychological theory.

Within a list that contains commas, you may need a semicolon. Before a list, you may need a colon or no punctuation at all; you will never need a semicolon before a list. Notice where we use semicolons and where we don't. We won't lead you astray.

Colons

Colons Are Required

Introducing lists

I have a bad feeling about his chances for success in college, given the *subjects that interest him most*: sex, drugs, and rock 'n' roll.

The sentence might have ended with the word *most*. The colon signaled that more information was on its way. Don't put a colon after any form of *to be* or *have*.

Introducing appositives

I changed my major from math to music to political science to modern languages to English before I ran into a big obstacle to further changes: *graduation*.

A dash might replace the colon if you were writing e-mail, greeting cards, or sentimental poetry to someone who won't correct its grammar and send it back to you. For anything more serious, the colon is the classy choice.

Introducing quotations and formal statements

I have written my own version of the Golden Rule: *It's easier to get forgiveness than permission.*

Notice that these two sentences are closely connected: the first introduces an idea, and the second presents it. The second sentence begins with a capital letter but does not begin with a coordinating conjunction; both of these are matters of taste, in this case, conservative taste.

Even for pompous people who spout mottoes and quote themselves, you separate the quotation from introductory material that is an independent clause. Had this person quoted the original Golden Rule, you would have punctuated it with a colon and quotation marks: "Do unto others as you would have them do unto you."

Between closely related independent clauses

> *This is a story,* I suppose, *about a failure in intelligence: the Rawlings' marriage was grounded in intelligence.* (Doris Lessing, "To Room Nineteen")

When the second clause summarizes, restates, or interprets the first clause, you may emphasize the close relationship between the clauses by using a colon. This is a stylistic choice, not a grammatical requirement. If your style favors three-piece suits with buttoned-up vests, begin the second clause with a capital letter.

With salutations of formal letters, between title and subtitle, to separate city from publisher and date in bibliographic entries, to indicate hours and minutes, and to show proportions

> Dear Dr. Frankenstein:

> Thank you for reviewing our book, *Inside Out: A Guide to Writing* (Boston: Allyn & Bacon, 1993). As of this writing (7:30, May 15, 1997), the proportion of positive to negative reviews is 4:1.

Colons Are Not Allowed
Between a verb and its object or complement

> The groupings for the show entries *will comprise beautiful breeds* such as hounds and retrievers.

The phrase "beautiful breeds" is the direct object of the verb *comprise*. Back in grade school, several teachers explained to you that transitive verbs—those that take direct objects—rely on their objects for completeness. They probably gave you an example like "Johnny hit the ball" and made you do exercises that you promptly forgot. See Grammar (pp. 175–176) if you have questions.

Between a preposition and its object

> The groupings for the show entries will be composed of *yappy breeds* such as terriers and working dogs.

The preposition is *of* and its object is *yappy breeds*. You've probably seen incorrectly punctuated lists in magazines and on signs often enough that you're not sure anymore where the colon goes. One place it doesn't go is between prepositions and their objects.

After *such as*

> The groupings for the show entries will include *breeds such as hounds,* terriers, and retrievers.

You use a colon when the grammar and sense of the sentence are completed without the material following the colon. The grammar and sense of the phrase *such as* are incomplete without the list that follows. You would use a colon if the sentence were phrased, "*The groupings for the show entries will include various breeds:* hounds, terriers, and retrievers." For some reason, people think that *such as* operates differently from other colon cases. It doesn't.

Apostrophes

Apostrophes Are Required

With contractions

> "Contrariwise," continued Tweedledee, "if it was so, it might be; and if it were so, it would be, but as it *isn't,* it *ain't. That's* logic." (Lewis Carroll, *Alice's Adventures in Wonderland*)

You don't need to be told that

- apostrophes replace omitted letters, or that

- in many formal contexts, such as research papers in the social sciences, you're not allowed to use contractions.

With possessives

"Why is it that at a *bachelor's* establishment the servants invariably drink the champagne?" (Oscar Wilde, *The Importance of Being Earnest*)

English will drive you right out of your mind if you insist on believing that language should be logical. But if you study the history of English (try Celia M. Millward's *A Biography of the English Language*, 2nd ed., Fort Worth: Harcourt Brace, 1996), you sometimes find that its inconsistent present comes from its interesting past. You may not be aware that in possessives, as well as contractions, the apostrophe shows that something is being replaced: in the case of possessives, the missing elements dropped out of the language long ago. Middle English retained endings from its Germanic roots, including possessives. Today we retain the ending but drop out a letter to facilitate speaking. Thus, Wilde writes "bachelor's establishment" rather than something like "bachelores establishment." The reason for the change is easy to hear when the phrase is spoken. The "bachelores establishment" is more difficult to say than the contraction, which makes "bachelor's" three syllables rather than four. The print conventions have regularized this form into all usage.

Of singular and plural nouns

A man's dying is more the *survivors'* affair than his own. (Thomas Mann, *The Magic Mountain*)

Singular nouns add an apostrophe -s to show possession. That should be the end of it, but it's not.

- Use only an apostrophe with words such as *appearance, conscience, righteousness* ("appearance' sake," "conscience' voice"), but pronounce the words as if you had added an apostrophe and -s.
- Use only an apostrophe with the names *Jesus* and *Moses* (it's traditional), and with names such as *Demosthenes* that contain two or more syllables and end in an unaccented syllable pronounced -eez.

- Plural nouns add only an apostrophe if the word ends in *-s.* If it doesn't end in *-s,* then add apostrophe *-s.* So you write "boys' books" while they're young, and "men's books" when they grow up.

Of compound words

I've been living in my *mother-in-law's* house since my divorce because I know he'll never find me here.

Add the apostrophe to the last syllable in hyphenated compounds such as *mother-in-law* and *editor-in-chief.* You don't want to think about the punctuation problems of trying to combine an apostrophe with a hyphen.

To show joint possession

Melanie, Ann, *and Serena's* portion of the inheritance will be a thousand dollars, divided equally except for that last penny.

Suppose you're writing your will. By putting the apostrophe *-s* on the last name, you imply joint possession (no, we're not implying anything about illegal drugs, but that's a very cute comment, and it's the first time we've heard it today); thus, you would give each person one-third of a thousand dollars. If you want to give them each one thousand dollars, give them each an apostrophe *-s.*

Melanie's, Ann's, and *Serena's* portion of the inheritance will be a thousand dollars.

Double-check the details with your lawyer, and ask him to send us a consultant's fee.

Plurals of letters, numbers, and words used as words

Speak your *t's* and *d's* clearly when you sing; learn your *8's* before you enter third grade; and don't use *you's* and *I's* in your geography report: no one promised you that second grade was going to be easy.

Exceptions: the *1940s, VIPs.*

Apostrophes Are Not Allowed

With possessive pronouns (*his, hers, its, ours, yours, theirs, whose*)

The little world of childhood with *its* familiar surroundings is a model of the greater world. (C. G. Jung, *Psychological Reflections: A Jung Anthology*)

No, it isn't logical that *its* is written without an apostrophe even though it's possessive. If this inconsistency annoys you, you can change the custom (that's what it is, a custom) when you become emperor of all the English-speaking peoples.

Meanwhile, if you really want to annoy an English teacher, try adding an apostrophe to the possessive pronoun its. To add insult to injury, protest when the teacher corrects it: say, "But it's possessive!"

With words that are not possessive

There are some *punctuations* [not *punctuation's*] that are interesting and there are some that are not. (Gertrude Stein)

Quotation Marks

Quotation Marks Are Required

To set off any words, spoken or written, taken directly from another

Actually, the correct version of the Biblical passage is not "*Pride goeth before a fall,*" but "*Pride goeth before destruction and a haughty spirit before a fall*" (Proverbs xvi.18).

Work quotations smoothly into the text. Don't say, "Here is Arnold Scharwarzenegger's opinion. According to Arnie . . . ." You want to create the impression that you've been quoting books since you were a baby, not that you just learned to read this afternoon. Build your sentence and paragraph so the quotation marks provide the only clue to a reader where your language leaves off and the quote begins.

- Each new paragraph of dialogue requires quotation marks before and after.

- Indent long quotations (more than a sentence) and omit the quotation marks. Many readers skip long quotations, so paraphrase unless you need the exact phrasing for its aesthetic effect or logical import.

With titles of short works and parts of long works

My favorite Beatles song, "Here Comes the Sun," from the album *Abbey Road,* has the goofiest lyrics the Beatles ever recorded.

In general, quotation marks enclose the titles of short works and sections of longer works, such as

- poems,
- short stories,
- songs,
- episodes of TV and radio programs,
- chapters or subdivisions of books, and
- magazine, journal, or newspaper articles.

The titles of longer works—books, magazines, newspapers, plays, and films—are italicized or underlined. See APA citation style (pp. 128–133) for variance from these customs.

With words referred to as words in certain contexts

Don't pronounce the *-l* sound in *palm* and *calm* unless you also pronounce it in *walk;* don't pronounce the *-n* in *kiln* unless you also pronounce it in *damn;* I don't even want to talk about the *-t* in *often.*

Italics, not quotation marks, customarily designate words as words in print. Use quotation marks if the context includes other kinds of italicized material such as foreign words or book titles.

After reading *Moby Dick,* I have just one question: What part of speech is "Moby"?

If your word processor's italics are illegible, use underlining or get a better word processor. If you can't underline or get a better word processor, use quotation marks and apologize.

When Quotation Marks Are Used with Other Punctuation Marks

With periods and commas at the ends of word groups

> "*Age and treachery,*" the old professor jeered, "*will always defeat youth and energy.*"

Periods and commas go inside the quotation marks. It's that simple.

Or it would be that simple if not for the Modern Language Association (MLA) parenthetical citation style. The quotation marks precede the citation and the end punctuation.

As Shakespeare observed, "Boil, boil, toil and trouble" (*Macbeth*).

With colons and semicolons at the ends of word groups

> The physicist announced, "*The flash point for my temper lowers in relation to the heat and noise in the room*"; she then looked daggers at the group sprawled in front of her fireplace.

Put colons and semicolons outside the quotation marks.

Why put colons and semicolons outside when periods and commas go inside the quotation marks? Choose the answer you like.

- This isn't a perfect world.
- It's a conspiracy by the CIA to cover up the Kennedy assassination.
- When women take over the world, we'll change that.
- Language isn't as orderly as we would like it to be.

With question marks and exclamation points

> The mathematician asked, "If 186,000 miles per second is the speed of light, *what's the speed of dark?*"
>
> *Are you surprised* his students say, "*This guy writes a mean test*"?

These marks follow the meaning of the sentence, going inside if they refer to the quoted material and outside if not. Check your sentence against the two examples.

- In the first example, the question mark goes inside the quotation marks because the quotation (The mathematician asked, *"If 186,000 miles per minute is the speed of light, what's the speed of dark?"*) is a question.

- In the second, the question mark goes outside the quotation marks because the quoted material is a statement (his students say, *"This guy writes a mean test"*) tucked inside a question (*"Are you surprised* [statement]"?).

- MLA style requires a period after the quotation marks when the question mark is inside the quotation marks. The resulting odd look will usually suggest rewriting the sentence.

As single quotation marks for quotations within quotations

She replied, **"**I agree with the comedienne who said, '*I think men who have a pierced ear are better prepared for marriage. They've experienced pain and bought jewelry.'***"**

Use single quotation marks—the apostrophe will do on most keyboards—for a quotation within a quotation. Americans should ignore the British practice of using single quotation marks for all quoted material; anytime you think it might be more tasteful to do something the British way, remember that the British boil their beef.

For an informal quotation within a sentence

My uncle has almost ruined my favorite Biblical quotation about seeing life *"through a glass darkly"* by misquoting it whenever he puts on his pink sunglasses.

Note that the source, the Bible, is included in the sentence, for the sake of courtesy to the reader and to avoid the appearance of plagiarism. If you're quoting an elegant phrase, don't mar its effect with ellipses,

commas, colons, and such. Just work it in with an air
of "Isn't it wonderful to be educated and able to drop
wise and witty phrases without any fuss," and surround
it with quotation marks. A combination of paraphrase,
informal quotation, and indirect quotation help, to
create an authoritative voice in your writing.

Quotation Marks Are Not Allowed

Around familiar expressions or humorous comments

> The sheriff's deputy *lost his cool* and handcuffed
> the young man for attempting a joke about *hick
> cops* and *bib overall uniforms.*

Writers who put quotation marks around a
clichéd phrase such as *lost his cool* might as well wear a
kick-me sign. This tells the reader, "I'm completely
unimaginative: not only am I using clichés, but I'm
also pointing them out to be sure you notice how
tediously I write." Putting humorous, ironic, or sarcastic comments in quotation marks is like poking
the reader in the ribs. "Hick cops and bib overall uniforms! That's a joke! Get it? Har, har!" Readers who
have a sense of humor will laugh if you make a funny
joke. If you're lucky, they'll ignore lame jokes. In either case, an understated delivery is more effective
than a clown suit.

Around indirect quotations

> I think it was Robert Benchley who said that *it
> took him fifteen years to discover he had no talent for
> writing, but by that time he was so famous that he
> couldn't give it up.*

Much of the original phrasing survives in indirect
quotation, so you have to be sure to credit your
source properly. You would use quotation marks if
you quoted the sentence exactly as it appears in Bart-
lett's *Familiar Quotations:*

> Robert Benchley remarked, "It took me fifteen
> years to discover that I had no talent for writing,
> but I couldn't give it up because by that time I
> was too famous."

Indirect quotation lends a muted, ironic tone to fiction writing. In nonfiction writing, indirect quotation can help the reader to shift smoothly from your original material to quoted material.

COMPUTER TIP

Check punctuation suggestions with another source.

- Grammar checkers are easily confused and often wrong about punctuation, especially commas. But you can't afford to ignore suggestions entirely.

- Use your grammar checker to help locate punctuation problems, and then check out the punctuation it suggests within this chapter.

Other Punctuation

Dashes

I'm worried about his health—*you know what a hypochondriac he is*—because he's suddenly stopped complaining.

Use dashes—when you want to create an impetuous, informal tone—as if they were commas, colons, or parentheses. The example illustrates how dashes can replace parentheses to enclose a long comment on the content of the rest of the sentence.

- "One thing worries me: his health" might be written "One thing worries me—his health."
- "One thing, his health, worries me" might be written as "One thing—his health—worries me."

If you are using a typewriter, you can use two hyphens to create a dash.

Parentheses

Parentheses enclose supplemental material, minor digressions, and afterthoughts.

My mother said (*as she was fond of saying*) that excuses satisfy those who make them.

Use parentheses to enclose letters or numbers labeling items in a series.

I'm telling you that (*a*) you should take out the garbage without complaining and (*2*) so there.

Of course, mixing your letters and your numbers detracts from the logical strength of your argument. Also, overusing parentheses creates an absent-minded air you probably want to avoid.

Brackets

Enclose in brackets any words or phrases inserted in word-for-word quotations.

How do I love thee?
[*Ummm*]
Let me count the ways.

Ellipses

Listening to the deejays report the news on the morning radio programs, I am sometimes reminded of Macbeth's famous observation that "*Life is a tale / Told by an idiot* . . . ."

Ellipses, three spaced periods indicating that material has been omitted from a quotation, remind the reader that material has been taken out of context. If you're quoting poetry, you insert a slash mark to indicate the end of the poetic line. You must enclose any other additions in brackets.

Ellipses are treated differently depending on where they occur.

- If the quoted material ends the sentence containing it, you add end punctuation: a fourth dot for a period, or an exclamation or question mark.
- If the quoted material begins the sentence containing it, you capitalize the first letter, enclosing that letter in brackets if the capital doesn't occur in the original (e.g., "'. . . [F]ull of sound and fury . . . '" describes most evenings at home with children: their sound, my fury.").

- If the quoted material occurs in the middle of the sentence containing it, add only the punctuation required by the context. "I'm sure I'll still be working on this paper 'Tomorrow and tomorrow and tomorrow . . . ,' and I'm rather afraid that in the end it will signify nothing."

- Using ellipses to indicate a thoughtful pause is about as stylish as leaving your fly unzipped. People whose attention you would like to attract will politely avert their eyes.

Slashes

Use a slash mark with a space before and after to indicate line breaks in quoted poetry that you choose to include in a line of prose.

> When asked whether he would babysit, he responded, "*The interest I take in my neighbor's nursery / Would have to grow to be even cursory.*"

Periods, Question Marks, and Exclamation Points

Shhh! Be vewy, vewy quiet. Can't you see I'm hunting wabbits? I wonder where that wascally wabbit has gone.

Ending with an exclamation point suggests emphasis, not necessarily shouting. End an unemphatic statement with a period. End direct questions with a question mark and indirect questions with a period.

COMPUTER TIP

Proofread in page view.

- If you are proofreading on screen, choose the page layout view. It focuses you on single lines of text more effectively than other views. If your word-processing program can zoom to a larger-than-life version of your text (say 125%), try zooming to slow yourself down so that you can concentrate on the details.

Proofreading Marks

Use proofreading marks to keep small changes from getting lost on the page. (If you need to rewrite a sentence completely while proofreading, it's usually easier to revise on screen or to rewrite the sentence on a sticky note and attach it to the text.)

Mark the changes in two places. Note the details of the change in the margin, and indicate the exact spot in the text where the change should go. Circle marginal words that are directions, so it's easy to distinguish the directions from words you want inserted into the text. Use slash marks to separate your marginal notes when you must make multiple changes in a single line.

Action	Mark in Margin	Mark in Text	Clean Copy
Delete	ℓ	The gene pool could use a a little chlorine.	The gene pool could use a little chlorine.
Insert	a	I didn't fight my way to the top of the food chain to be vegetarian. ^	I didn't fight my way to the top of the food chain to be a vegetarian.
Replace a letter	z	Black holes are where God divided by zero.	Black holes are where God divided by zero.
Oops, don't delete	(stet)	Give me ambiguity or give me something else.	Give me ambiguity or give me something else.
Transpose	(tr)	Always remember, you're just/unique, like everyone else.	Always remember, you're unique, just like everyone else.

Action	Mark in Margin	Mark in Text	Clean Copy
New para-graph	¶	Forget about world peace. Visu-alize using your turn signal.	Forget about world peace. Visualize using your turn signal.
No para-graph (run in)	run in	Very funny, Scotty. Now beam down my clothes.	Very funny, Scotty. Now beam down my clothes.
Capital-ize	cap	Diplomacy is the art of saying, "nice doggie!" till you can find a rock.	Diplomacy is the art of saying, "Nice doggie!" till you can find a rock.
Lower-case	lc	He who laughs Last thinks SLOWEST.	He who laughs last thinks slowest.
Spell out	sp	There are 3 kinds of people: those who can count and those who can't.	There are three kinds of people: those who can count and those who can't.
Close up space	⌒	Why is abbreviation suc h a long word?	Why is abbreviation such a long word?
Insert space	#	Women who seek tobe equal with men lack ambition.	Women who seek to be equal with men lack ambition.

Action	Mark in Margin	Mark in Text	Clean Copy
Insert comma		According to my calcula- tions‸the problem doesn't exist.	According to my calcula- tions, the problem doesn't exist.
Insert period		Time is what keeps things from hap- pening all at once‸	Time is what keeps things from hap- pening all at once.
Insert colon		Lottery‸a tax on people who are bad at math.	Lottery: a tax on people who are bad at math.
Insert semi- colon		Few women admit their age‸few men act it.	Few women admit their age; few men act it.
Insert apos- trophe		I smile be- cause I don't know whats going on.‸	I smile be- cause I don't know what's going on.
Insert quota- tion marks		‸Auntie Em: Hate you, hate Kansas, taking the dog.‸ —Dorothy	"Auntie Em: Hate you, hate Kansas, taking the dog." —Dorothy
Insert paren- theses		Lead me not into tempta- tion‸I can find it myself‸	Lead me not into tempta- tion (I can find it myself).

Action	Mark in Margin	Mark in Text	Clean Copy
Insert en dash	$\frac{/}{N}$	I like you, but I wouldn't want to see you working with sub≠atomic particles.	I like you, but I wouldn't want to see you working with sub–atomic particles.
Insert em dash	$\frac{/}{m}$	Conscious-ness‚that annoying time between naps.	Conscious-ness—that annoying time between naps.
Boldface	(bf)	Warning: Dates on cal-endar are closer than they appear.	**Warning:** Dates on cal-endar are closer than they appear.
Remove boldface (use roman type)	(rom)	We are Microsoft. Resistance is futile. You will be **assimilated.**	We are Microsoft. Resistance is futile. You will be assimilated.
Italicize	(ital)	Make it idiot-proof, and someone will make a better idiot.	*Make it idiot-proof,* and someone will make a better idiot.
Remove italics (use roman type)	(rom)	*Eschew obfuscation.*	Eschew obfuscation.

Details, Details

It's a damn poor mind that can think of only
one way to spell a word!

(Attributed to Andrew Jackson)

The Customs of Print

The printing press, which blessed us with access to
the books we could hardly live without, also cursed
us with the concepts of correct spelling and mechanics. Before the printing press, people spelled
phonetically or according to whim, and some of
them scarcely bothered at all with mechanical details or even punctuation. As soon as multiple
copies of a single work (such as Gutenberg's Bible)
appeared, people got used to seeing a text printed a
certain way, and they got fussy about customs, as
people will. Standardized spelling and mechanics
ensued, to writers' perpetual discomfort.

Sensible Spelling

Where spelling is concerned, you should choose your
parents carefully: make sure at least one has a gene
for photographic memory. If you must use other criteria to choose your parents, the best help anyone
can offer you is the spell checker. Spell checkers will
miss some words, though, so human eyes continue to
be important, especially eyes that belong to people

with a lot of reading and writing experience. There's a quaint old device called a dictionary that is useful. A few rules may also help some spellers.

Spelling Rules

1. Use *i* before *e* except after *c* or when sounded like *a* as in *neighbor* or *weigh*.

   Exceptions: *neither/either, seize, weird, leisure, foreign*.

2. Drop a final silent *e* before adding a suffix (unless the suffix begins with a consonant): *excite, exciting* but *excitement*.

   Argument and *judgment* are exceptions in American English; they are spelled with an *e* in British English. *Changeable* and *truly* are exceptions on both sides of the Atlantic.

3. To add *-s* or *-ed* to a word ending in *-y*, change the *y* to *i* when following a consonant but leave as is following a vowel: *copy, copied* but *enjoy, enjoyed*. Never change the *y* to *i* for a proper name: the *Sweeny* family, the *Sweenys*.

4. For a word ending in a consonant, double the consonant when a single vowel precedes the consonant and when the syllable before the consonant is accented: *get, getting* but *benefit, benefited*.

5. To make plurals, add *-s* to most nouns unless they end in *s* or *z* sounds (*s, x, sh, ch*): *cats* but *boxes*.

   Add *-s* to nouns ending in *o* after vowels and *-es* after consonants (musical words are an exception): *folios, zeroes* but *pianos*.

   Hyphenated nouns require an *-s* after the emphasized word: *justices*-of-the-peace.

   Foreign words used as English words generally follow the plural form of their original languages: *medium, media* or *beau, beaux*.

ESL note (see 2 above) Spellings vary among English-speaking countries, which may cause confusion when you are moving from one English-speaking country to another. Consult a dictionary when in doubt. Example: *realize* [American] but *realise* [British].

If Stephen King Wrote a Spelling Test
(Frequently Misspelled Words)

academic	decision	laboratory
accidentally	definitely	license
accommodate	describe	maneuver
acknowledge	description	mathematics
acquire	desperate	mischievous
across	develop	necessary
all right	disappear	noticeable
altogether	disappoint	occasionally
amateur	disastrous	occurred
analyze	dissatisfied	omitted
apparently	embarrass	optimistic
appearance	eminent	pamphlet
appropriate	emphasize	parallel
argument	entirely	particularly
arrangement	environment	pastime
athlete	especially	perspiration
attendance	exaggerated	phenomenon
audience	exhaust	physically
basically	existence	playwright
believe	familiar	politics
benefited	fascinate	practically
bureau	February	precede
business	flattery	preferred
calendar	foreign	prejudice
candidate	government	privilege
changeable	grammar	proceed
characteristic	grammarian	professor
commitment	guidance	pronunciation
committed	harass	quiet
committee	height	quite
competitive	illiterate	recommend
conceivable	incidentally	reference
conferred	incredible	referred
conscience	inevitable	repetition
conscious	irrelevant	restaurant
curiosity	irresistible	rhythm
dear	knowledge	sandwich

schedule	succeed	vacuum
secretary	surprise	vengeance
seize	thorough	villain
separate	tragedy	weird
similar	transferred	whether
sincerely	truly	writing
sophomore	unnecessarily	
subtly	usually	

Miscellaneous Mechanics

Capitalization

Proper nouns are capitalized; common nouns are not. Proper nouns name specific persons, places, things, or concepts.

Proper Nouns	*Common Nouns*
Felix	cat
Illinois Symphony	symphony orchestra
President Lincoln	the president
the Age of Innocence	an innocent
the Isle of Innisfree	the isle of fantasy
Illinois State University	university
the Victorian Era	the late nineteenth century
Newton's Law	the law of gravity
Mother Teresa	her mother

Capitals are required

Category	*Example*
degrees	Ph.D., Ll.D.
deities	Minerva
departments	Department of Foreign Languages
designated family members	Dad, Mom
documents	The Declaration of Independence
educational institutions	Illinois State University
events	the Civil War

Category	Example
historical movements	the Temperance Movement
nationalities and languages	Swiss, German
particular courses	English 101
periods	the Renaissance
political parties	Libertarian
races	Asian, Native American
religions and followers	Mohammedanism, Christians
school subject names, if they are languages	English, French
specific places	Woodstock
tribes	Iroquois
months, days of the week, holidays	October, Sunday, Reformation Sunday

Capitals are not allowed

Category	Example
seasons	fall
dates of the month	the tenth of this month
school subject names that are not languages	history, psychology

A few complications

Titles of honor or designation   Titles are capitalized when used with names but not when used alone.

Dr. Evans, *Pastor* Wells, *Sister* Wendy

The *pastor* stammered and blushed when he read from the *Song of Songs*.

Usage can vary when the reference is specific.

Ask *Pastor* to join the altos in the jacuzzi.

Titles of works   In titles and subtitles of works such as books, songs, or articles, major words (including those following hyphens) should be capitalized.

The House of Mirth

"Comin' through the Rye"

The History of D-Day

First word of a sentence or quoted sentence   The exception to this custom lies in the use of a fused quotation.

My father always said that of his life experiences *"raising children was the most fulfilling,"* but he seemed to prefer his cars for company.

A capital does not follow explanatory interruptions in quotations.

"Quit teasing your sister," she warned, *"or* fur will grow on your ears."

Following a colon   No capital follows a colon unless a complete clause follows the colon; then the capital is optional.

Read these books before college: *Moby Dick, War and Peace,* and *Middlemarch.* You [you] may then quote from them to seem wise.

COMPUTER TIP

Set up the change case function of your word-processing program to handle capitalization.

- As you begin writing ordinary sentences and paragraphs, use "sentence case." Switch to "lower case" for lists. The title case setting may incorrectly capitalize unimportant words such as articles and pronouns.

Abbreviations

Good abbreviations

Capitalize abbreviated names of agencies or organizations:

SPCA, CIA, TV 10, IBM

Titles before or after proper names:

Dr. Sandra Phelps	John Witherspoon, Sr.
Ms. Anne Smith	Curt White, Ph.D.
Fr. Andrew Walters	Bruce Dietz, D.D.S.

When using an abbreviation that the reader is unlikely to know, write out the referent in full in parentheses the first time it is used in the document: SCA (Society for Creative Anachronism). Don't bother if you aren't going to refer to the SCA again.

Commonly accepted abbreviations include B.C. (before Christ) or B.C.E. (before the Common Era) and A.D. ("anno Domini") or C.E. (Common Era). A.M. and P.M. must accompany a figure: 1 A.M. (but *in the afternoon,* not *in the P.M.*).

Bad and ugly abbreviations

Category	Example
Personal names	Janice (not Janie)
Titles when used without the name	Her biology *professor* [not *prof.*] often worked in the lab for hours after class.
Units	*inch* [not *in.*]
Holidays	*Christmas* [not *Xmas*]
Days of the week	*Tuesday* [not *Tues.* or *T*]
Months	*October* [not *Oct.*]
Courses of study	*English degree* [not *Eng. deg.*]
Divisions of written work	*chapter* [not *ch.*]
States and countries	*Illinois* [not *Ill.* or *IL*]
Business names	*State Farm* [not *St. Fm.*]

To abbreviate or not to abbreviate
Abbreviations, much loved by bureaucrats and other enemies of truth and beauty, serve the typist rather than the reader. Be very careful with them.

Latin   Use Latin abbreviations for informal writing, but write out the English phrase in formal writing.

English	Latin	Abbreviation
for example	exempla gratia	e.g.
and so forth	et cetera	etc.
that is	id est	i.e.
note well	nota bene	N.B.
compare	confer	cf.
and others	et alia	et al.

Numbers   Spell out numbers of one or two numerals.

Brandon is *three* years old.

Bear is *twenty-seven* dog years old.

Use figures for numbers of more than two numerals.

We ordered *358* tulip bulbs, which, we realized too late, required that we dig *358* individual holes in the ground.

Avoid beginning a sentence with a number because you'll have to write out the number to capitalize it.

One hundred sixty-five is as fast as my Corvette will go.

Note that some technical writing formats require that numbers always be shown as numerals.

Are there exceptions and complications? *Mais certainement!*

It is generally acceptable to use numbers in the following situations:

Dates	June 12, 1943, 1100 A.D.
Time of day	3:04 P.M.
Addresses	4240 English, ISU, Normal, IL 61790-4240
Percentages, fractions, decimals	33 percent (or 33%), 1/3, .33333
Statistics	population size of 300
Surveys	10 zones surveyed
Scores	love 15
Exact amounts of money	$55.23
Divisions of books, plays	volume 2, Act 2
Identification numbers	Social Security # 000–00–0000

Italics and Underlining

Printed material

The general rule suggests that a complete work is italicized or underlined; one that can be included in a collection or volume is placed in quotation marks (see Punctuation, p. 91).

Titles of books	*Hard Times*
Plays	*The Importance of Being Earnest*
Films	*The Blues Brothers*
Television programs	*X-Files*
Radio programs	*Evening Edition*
Musical compositions	*Porgy and Bess*
Choreographic works	Janet Heyslip's *Night Watch*
Works of visual art	Frank Young's *Beyond Centaurus*
Long poems	*The Ring and the Book*
Magazines and journals	*Harpers, College English*
Pamphlets	*Training Puppies*
Comic strips	*Doonesbury*
Software	*Microsoft Word*

Aircraft, trains, and ships

These are the voyages of the starship *Enterprise.*

I'm ridin' on the *City of New Orleans.*

We sailed on the sloop *John B.*

Foreign words

Italicize (or underline) unless you can find the word written without italics in a recent English dictionary.

You call them *hors d'oeuvres;* I call them bait on a cracker.

Words, letters, and numbers

Italicize (or use quotation marks around) words used as words, letters used as letters, and numbers used as numbers.

In *Monty Python and the Holy Grail,* the knights say *nih.*

The choir stopped pronouncing *-r* when the director told them they sounded like a backup group for Willie Nelson.

In Chicago, everyone wants the jersey with the number *23*.

Emphasis

Don't underline or italicize for emphasis. Just don't. (Repetition is more effective.)

COMPUTER TIP

Beware of italics.

- Though most word-processing programs will produce italics, the italics often throw off spacing, causing your italicized words to lean drunkenly against their neighbors. You can use underlining to substitute for italics, but note that the underline should not extend across spaces between words.

Hyphens

Divide words with hyphens only when necessary and then only in the middle of words.

Do not leave one letter and a hyphen on one line.

Divide at syllables: *evi-dent,* not *e-vident* or *evid-ent.*

Divide compound words at the hyphen break that already exists.

Compound nouns may be written as one word, as a hyphenated form, or as two words: *laptop, watt-hour, kitchen sink.* Consult a dictionary when in doubt. Always write the compound as two words if there is no listing.

Hyphens connect two or more words that function as one adjective before a noun.

The class worked, with no idea why they were doing it, on the *sentence-combining* exercise.

The children rolled their eyes toward heaven as Dad started in on his *often-told* tales.

Some phrases drop the hyphen when they function as a noun or a verb.

The class likes to do *sentence combining.*

Grandfather *often told* us stories.

Don't create hyphenated compounds using *-ly* words.

She seemed to have learned the twenty habits of *highly ineffective* people.

Hyphens may be used to avoid ambiguity or confusion, as in *recreation* (in the vacation sense) as opposed to *re-creation* (in the doing-it-over sense).

Hyphens may also break up words with hard-to-read double letters: *anti-inflammatory*.

Hyphens follow *ex-*, *self-*, and *all-*, and precede *-elect*.

Hyphens form fractions and numbers from twenty-one to ninety-nine.

For more details on hyphens than you could ever imagine, refer to the *Chicago Manual of Style*.

COMPUTER TIP

Check hyphenated words in a recent dictionary.

• The spell checker will let you murder the language with hyphens, so don't trust it. Look up hyphenated words in a recent dictionary; usage may have changed since you last checked.

CHAPTER

5

Your Documentation, Please

> There is nothing more miserable in the world
> than to arrive in paradise and look like your
> passport photo.
>
> (Erma Bombeck)

Documentation allows a reader to find answers to some questions that arise naturally during reading. Who wrote that? Where and when was it published? Answering these questions, in effect, answers another, unspoken question that readers have, not about your writing but about you. The question is, "No offense intended, but do you know what you're doing? Do you know the legalities and courtesies of traveling in the world of books?" Your documentation acts as your credentials, your passport to academic respectability. Academic disciplines use a number of documentation styles, three of which are covered here: the Modern Language Association (MLA), the American Psychological Association (APA), and the *Chicago Manual of Style* (CMS).

Readers will occasionally overlook problems of documentation, but teachers and editors are a different matter altogether: it is wise to take care—ask questions or locate published examples of the style—to discover which format is expected. To see a kindhearted, helpful teacher turn into a border guard with an attitude, try submitting a piece of writing with messy citations or without a works cited page.

MLA

In-Text Citation

1. Author named in text

An author may be referenced within the text with page numbers noted at the end of the reference:

> Joe Stuessy notes that the Grateful Dead were once known as the Warlocks (242).

2. Author not named in text

Where the information is foremost or the author has been noted earlier, the name and page numbers may appear in parentheses:

> The fact that the Dead never had a Top 40 hit (Stuessy 243) is the clearest proof that popular taste and bad taste are the same thing.

3. Two or three authors

Treat two or three authors as one with the names appearing either in the text or in parentheses:

> Scharton and Neuleib note that writers pay intellectual debts by acknowledging sources (295), however much trouble it is to figure out the format of citations.

4. Four or more authors

The first author may be named in the text, noting co-authors, or the first author's name with *et al.* (abbreviation for Latin *et alia,* "and others") may be placed in parentheses:

> College students can help high school students with their writing (Duin et al. 147).

5. Unknown author

Note the title in the text or refer to a short form in parentheses:

> The unknown poet creates a green world (*Sir Gawain*).

6. Corporate author

Name the corporate author in either the text or in parentheses:

> The National Council of Teachers of English
> notes that video portfolios are available to
> teachers for their review and use (9).

7. Two or more works by one author

Where two or more works by one author are listed in the works cited, name the work in the text, or include a short form of the title in parentheses:

> *In Rock and Roll: Its History and Stylistic*
> *Development*, Stuessy summarizes information
> on classical style covered in his earlier
> book (148).

If author and shortened form must both appear in parentheses, follow this form:

> (Stuessy, *Rock and Roll* 148)

8. A source quoted in another source

Place the abbreviation *qtd. in* to indicate that one author is quoting another:

> Dylan's jacket notes for one record are unclear
> and illogical: "The first one had a broken nose,
> the second a broken arm, and the third was
> broke" (qtd. in Stuessy 191).

9. Novel, play, or poem

Give information for a specific edition, but add information that will apply to different editions as well.

For a novel, note the part or chapter.

> In *Till We Have Faces*, the main character,
> who has little imagination and less experience
> of lovers, mistakenly says, "Nothing that is
> beautiful hides its face" (141; ch. 14).

For a play, list act, scene, and, if the edition you are using provides them, line numbers. Use Arabic numerals.

"A handbag!" rages Lady Bracknall, when she learns that her niece's fiance lists a piece of luggage as his place of birth (*The Importance of Being Earnest*, 5.1).

For a poem, cite the part (if applicable) and line numbers.

"Did you see this ring / Tis Roman work" begins *The Ring and the Book* (1.414).

10. Work in an anthology
The name of the author of the work is cited, not that of the editor of the anthology:

In his essay "On Fairy Stories," Tolkien contends that "[b]ooks written entirely for children are poor even as children's books" (59), which demonstrates that even a good writer and a wise man can overgeneralize.

11. Entire work
Use the author's name in the text or in parentheses:

Shor's work on Freire introduced the South American thinker to North American scholars, a number of whom promptly set about trying to use ideas developed in desperately poor and oppressed Third World cultures to teach American teenagers who were reared in malls.

12. Multivolume work
When more than one volume is cited, note the volume number in parentheses, followed by the page number.

Beethoven's symphonies supposed smaller orchestras and longer attention spans than we often see in modern concerts (Blom 2: 314).

13. Two or more works
To cite two or more sources on a single point, separate the sources with a semicolon:

Despite what your mother told you about love changing people, sources on personality theory tend to agree on the constant nature of individual traits (Kroeger and Thuesen 11; Keirsey and Bates 4).

14. Authors with the same last name

Include the first name of the author to clarify the reference:

C. S. Lewis and Warnie Lewis, his rather dull and dorky brother, have both written about their life together (C. S. Lewis 534).

15. Work without page numbers

Page numbers need not be listed for works with unnumbered pages or of one page or from an alphabetized source. Electronic citations may note paragraphs:

Insite/Out begins with several references to other activity sites (Scharton, par. 1).

> ### COMPUTER TIP
>
> Use the ruler to create hanging indents for works cited pages.
>
> • Use the ruler bar to format your footnotes, endnotes, and works cited. You can create a hanging indent by dragging the bottom half of the indent marker to the indent point.

Works Cited

Books

1. One author

Lewis, C. S. *Till We Have Faces.* New York: Time/Life, 1956.

2. Two or three authors

Kroeger, Otto, and Janet M. Thuesen. *Type Talk.* New York: Delacorte, 1988.

3. Editor

   Lewis, C. S., ed. *Essays Presented to Charles Williams.*
   Grand Rapids: Eerdmans, 1966.

4. Author with editor

   Hooper, Walter, ed. *The Letters of C. S. Lewis to
   Arthur Greeves (1946–1963).* New York:
   Macmillan, 1979.

5. More than two authors or editors

   Gilligan, Carol, et al., eds. *Women, Girls, and
   Psychotherapy: Reframing Resistance.* New York:
   Haworth, 1991.

6. Unknown author

   Beowulf. Trans. Kevin Crossley-Holland. New
   York: Farrar, 1968.

7. Corporate author

   American Express. *Investors Guide.* New York:
   AmEx, 1997.

8. Two or more works by the same author

   Hope, Laura Lee. *The Bobbsey Twins.* New York:
   Grosset, 1950.

   —. *The Bobbsey Twins in the Country.* Racine:
   Whitman, 1950.

9. Translation

   Camus, Albert. *The Stranger.* Trans. Stuart Gilbert.
   New York: Vintage, 1946.

10. Reprint of an earlier edition

    Whitman, Walt. *Leaves of Grass.* 1855. New York:
    Viking, 1959.

11. Revised edition

    Stuessy, Joe. *Rock and Roll: Its History and Stylistic
    Development.* 2nd ed. Englewood Cliffs:
    Prentice, 1994.

12. Work in several volumes

Blom, Eric, ed. *Grove's Dictionary of Music and Musicians.* 5th ed. 10 vols. New York: St. Martin's, 1961.

13. Essay in an anthology

Tolkien, J. R. R. "On Fairy Stories." *Essays Presented to Charles Williams.* Ed. C. S. Lewis. Grand Rapids: Eerdmans, 1966. 38-89.

14. Poem in an anthology

Browning, Robert. "The Ring and the Book." *The Complete Poetical Works of Browning.* Ed. Horace E. Scudder. Boston: Houghton, 1895. 414-601.

15. Preface or introduction

Tolkien, Christopher. Introduction. *Unfinished Tales of Numenor and Middle-Earth.* By J. R. R. Tolkien. Ed. Christopher Tolkien. Boston: Houghton, 1980. 3-15.

Periodicals

16. Newspaper article
(Signed)

Manes, Stephen. "A Pocketful of Dreams and Bytes." *New York Times* 16 Sept. 1997: B13.

(Unsigned)

"New Video-Based Programs for Secondary Teachers." *Council Chronicle* Sept. 1997: 9.

17. Magazine articles with no volume number
(Signed)

Goldsmith, Jeffrey. "The Last Human Chessmaster." *Wired* Feb. 1995: 120-23.

(Unsigned)

"Earthbound Telescopes Take on Hubble." *Scientific American* Nov. 1991: 121.

18. Periodical articles

(Periodical with continuous page numbering)

Faigley, Lester. "Literacy after the Revolution."
   College Composition and Communication 48
   (1997): 30-43.

(Periodical with each issue paged separately)

Mohr, Marian M. "Teacher-Researcher at Work."
   English Journal 83.6 (1994): 19-21. [vol. 83,
   issue 6]

Other sources

19. Article from a reference book

"Emily Elizabeth Dickinson." *Dictionary of American Biography.* 1964.

20. Anonymous pamphlet

Aaron Copland: A Catalogue of His Works. New
   York: Boosey, n.d.

21. The Bible

The Dartmouth Bible. Boston: Houghton, 1961.

List any Bible version other than the King James.
Cite book, chapter, and verse in parentheses in the
text of your paper this way: (Matt. 12.1-3). Underline
only the titles of bibles other than the King James
version.

22. A letter in a published collection

Lewis, C. S. Letter of 20 March 1929. *Letters of
   C. S. Lewis to Arthur Greeves.* Ed. Walter
   Hooper. New York: Macmillan, 1979.

23. An unpublished or personal letter

Lewis, C. S. Letter to an anonymous lady. 4 June
   1941. Lewis Archives. Wheaton College,
   Wheaton, IL.

24. Personal or telephone interview

Palm, Marian. Personal interview. 1 Sept. 1997.

25. Review

(Signed)

> Hoffman, Daniel. "Life Was One Long
> Midnight." Rev. of *Life of Edgar A. Poe* by
> Kenneth Silverman. *New York Times Book
> Review* 22 Dec. 1991: 1+.

(Unsigned)

> Rev. of *JFK*. *Chicago Tribune* 26 Dec. 1991,
> sec. 1: 10.

26. Film

> Spielberg, Stephen, dir. *Star Wars*. Perf. Carrie
> Fisher and Harrison Ford. Warner Brothers,
> 1978.

27. Lecture

> Getsi, Lucia. "Chasing the Still Unravished
> Bride." Illinois State U. Distinguished
> Professor Lecture. Normal. 6 Nov. 1997.

28. Record, Tape, or CD

> Whelan, John. *Celtic Reflections*. Narada, 1996.

29. Published proceedings of a conference

> Chan Kai Yau. *Report of the Regional Seminar on
> Evaluation and Measurement. Singapore 1980.*
> Singapore: SEAMEO, 1980.

CD-ROM and online sources

30. E-mail or newsgroup

> Dozier, Kim. "Report on Mentoring." E-mail to
> Janice Neuleib. 31 Oct. 1997.

31. CD-ROM

Give complete information for nonelectronic
source and pertinent information for electronic
source.

(Single edition)

> *Quicken Deluxe.* CD-ROM. Vers. 6. Menlo Park: Intuit, 1995.

(Series)

> *1998 Worldbook Multimedia Encyclopedia.* CD-ROM. 2 discs. San Diego: IVID, 1998.

(Instructional text)

> *Fender Guitar 101.* CD-ROM. San Francisco: Lyrrus, 1994.

32. Online material

> Neuleib, Janice. "Writing Committee Proposal." Online posting. 13 Oct. 1997. English Department Listserv. Illinois State U. <jneuleib@ilsta.edu>

33. World Wide Web

> Scharton, Maurice. *Insite/Out: Resources for Rhetoric and Writing.* 25 Mar. 2001. <www.ilstu.edu/scharton>

34. Online material from a computer network

> Hatfield, Edward, and Susan Sprecher. "Men's and Women's Preferences in Marital Partners in the United States, Russia, and Japan." *Journal of Cross-Cultural Psychology* 26.6 (Nov. 1995): 1 Sept. 1997 <www.milner.ilstu.edu>

MLA style site

> Online citations
> <www.mla.org/style/style_nav.htm>

Scholarly project

> Dickens Project John O. Jordan, Ed. Jan. 1981. U of California, Santa Cruz 9 Sept. 2000 <humwww.ucsc.edu/dickens/>

Professional site

Teaching Materials Center. Illinois SU.
4 Sept. 2000 <www.mlb.ilstu.edu/
about/depts/tmc/home.htm>

Personal site

Scharton, Maurice. Home page. 9 Sept. 2000
<www.ilstu.edu/~scharton/>

Book

Dickens, C[harles]. Bleak House. London, 1853.
Dickens Project. Ed. JoAnna Rottke.
Jan. 1999. U Cal Santa Cruz. 8 Sept. 2000.
<humwww.ucsc.edu/dickens/searchworks/
BleakHouse/BH.html>

Poem

Parker, D[orothy]. "A Very Short Song." *Enough
Rope.* New York, 1940. Dorothy Parker Home
Page. Ed. Kevin Fitzpatrick. July 2000.
Algonquin Society. 9 Sept. 2000.
<www.bway.net/~kfitz/parker.htm>

Article in a reference database

"Behemoth." 1989. Oxford English Dictionary.
2 Oct. 2000. <dictionary.oed.com/cgi/
entry/00019683>

Online database

Hosker, Gary. "Afghan Hounds." The
Encyclopedia of the Lurcher/Staghound.
6 Oct. 2000. <www.users.daelnet.co.uk/
lurchers/encyclopedia.htm>

**Article in a journal with continuous
pagination throughout the annual volume**

Bigelow, Gordon. "Market Indicators: Banking
and Domesticity in Dickens's Bleak House."
English Literary History 67.2 (2000) 589-615

<muse.jhu.edu/journals/elh/v067/
67.2bigelow.html>

Article in a journal that pages issues separately

Smith, Victoria. "A Story Beside(s) Itself:
The language of loss in Djuna Barne's
Nightwood." *PMLA* 114.2 (1999):18 pars.
12 Jan. 1999. <newfirstsearch.oclc.org:80/
WebZ/

Article in a newspaper

Young, Ken. "Ideal home makes perfect office."
IT Week, 25 Sept 2000, v3 i36 p64
<web6.infotrac.galegroup.com/itw/
infomark/449/121/37381737w3/
purl=rc8_CDB_su_hemingway,+wayne>

Article in a magazine

Timothy, Noah. "Confessions of a Paul Simon
Fan." Slate 3 Oct. 2000. 4 Oct. 2000.
<slate.msn.com/Code/chatterbox/chatter
box.asp?Show=10/3/2000&idMessage =6188>

Posting to a discussion list

Thomas, Kari. "Cleaning Bulldog Ears." Online
posting. 28 April 2000. I-Dog. 6 Oct. 2000.
<www.i-dog.com/board/>

COMPUTER TIP

Bookmark sites where you find information.

- Use your browser's "bookmark" or "add to favorites" function to keep track of sites where you find information.
- While you're there, copy the URL from the address line in your web browser, and paste it into the document you're working on. Add the date you visited the site.

MLA Manuscript Format

These standards are arbitrary, and you may be forgiven if you feel like the victim of fraternity hazing. But you must suffer the rituals if you want to belong to the club.

Title and identification
Instructors and publishers will specify title pages, but if none is required, place name, date, and course information in the upper left-hand corner of the first page. Double-space between lines, and double-space before the title, which is centered.

Margins, indentation, and spacing
Leave at least one-inch margins, use five spaces for a paragraph indent, and double-space the text. Quotations longer than four typed lines should be set apart from the text and indented ten spaces.

COMPUTER TIP

Use your computer for easy formatting.

- By using the page setup and format functions of your word-processing program, you can set margins, line spacing, and first line indents (1/2 inch is good).

Page numbers
Place page numbers in the upper right-hand corner, one-half inch from the top of the paper. Use your last name or a short title before the number for identification, unless the paper is being submitted for blind review.

Punctuation and spacing
Leave one space after all punctuation, except for end punctuation (periods, question and exclamation marks). MLA allows either single or double space after end punctuation. Form an em dash with two hyphens, using no spaces. If you are using a computer, use the insert symbol function to insert the dash.

Works Cited
The page begins with the title "Works Cited," centered, and entries are alphabetized. For second

and subsequent uses of the same author's name in the list, use three hyphens. Turn lines indent five spaces.

APA

The American Psychological Association documentation style is used in social science and education. Like MLA style, APA style requires in-text citation instead of footnotes. Also like MLA, APA seems intended to test your patience. Be absolutely sure you're using the right style the first time. Having to change from MLA to APA has been known to bring on weeping fits.

Differences:

1. APA does not spell out the author's first names.
2. APA lists the date just after the author's name.
3. APA does not cite page numbers except when a direct quotation is used; then the APA style includes the page number in the in-text citation.
4. APA treats titles as if they were ordinary sentences, capitalizing only the first word of a title, the first word following a colon within a title, and proper names.
5. APA uses a comma to separate the year of publication and the page numbers, whereas MLA uses no punctuation.
6. MLA uses hanging indention for citations; APA uses paragraph indentation. APA titles the section "References."
7. APA uses ampersands in references and in-text citations.
8. The *Publication Manual of the APA*, fourth edition, on page 194, explains that "Just as a double-spaced manuscript page is typeset as a single-spaced printed page, the paragraph indent in a reference entry will be converted to a hanging indent when typeset." Thus the student paper in this text follows the example on pp. 265–266 of the APA Manual, presenting the references with paragraph indent and understanding that a typesetter would change the double space to single space and the paragraph indentation to hanging indentation.

APA In-Text Citation

1. Paraphrase

Mention your source within the text of your paper or in parentheses:

> Stolarek (1994) noted that novice writers work best from models.

> When teachers write or speak, they should keep in mind that novice writers work best from models (Stolarek, 1994).

2. Quotation

Introduce the quotation with the author's name and the source's date:

> Faigley (1992) maintains that "the ideal of community privileges face-to-face relations as the primary form of social interaction" (p. 231), which is a professorial way of saying that people who live together prefer to talk to one another.

3. Two authors

Use "and" in running text and "&" in parenthetical references:

> It is astonishing to learn how recently Lunsford and Ede (1982) began the discussion of audience among scholars of composition.

> Audience as a formal topic was introduced by two authors in conversation (Lunsford & Ede, 1982).

4. Three to five authors

Use all authors' names in the first citation and the first author followed by "et al." in following references. Do not underline or italicize "et al."

> (Neuleib, Cain, Ruffus, & Scharton, 1998)

5. Six or more authors

The first author's name is always used alone, followed by "et al."

> (Lewis et al., 1998)

6. Corporate authors
Abbreviate after the first reference:

> (The State Farm Automobile Insurance
> Company [State Farm Auto], 1997)

Later citations:
> (State Farm Auto, 1997.)

7. Authors with the same last name
To avoid confusion, use initials:

> (K. King, 1967)

8. Unknown author
Use the complete title or a clear partial title:
("Farmer's Life," 1855). Underline or italicize books
and put articles in quotation marks. Treat an anony-
mous author as if "anonymous" were a name:
(Anonymous, 1980).

9. Personal communications
Cite in text by initials and last name with date: (J. C.
Hook, personal communication, October 7, 1967).
Do not list in references.

References

Use the word "References" to head the list of sources.

Books

1. Basic book format
> Tannen, D. (1986). *That's not what I meant!*
> New York: Ballantine.

2. Two or more authors
> Phelps, L. W., & Emig, J. (1995). *Feminine
> principles and women's experience in American
> composition and rhetoric.* Pittsburgh:
> University of Pittsburgh Press.

3. Corporate author
> Illinois State University. (1997). *Facts 1997-98.*
> Normal: Author.

4. Unknown author

   Grammar hotline directory 1995. (1995). Virginia
   Beach: Tidewater Community College.

5. Editor

   Hooper, W. (Ed.). (1979). *The letters of C. S. Lewis
   to Arthur Greeves.* New York: Macmillan.

6. Edition other than the first

   Ramage, J. D., & Bean, J. C. (1998). *Writing
   arguments: A rhetoric with readings* (4th ed.).
   Boston: Allyn & Bacon.

7. Translation

   Tolstoy, L. N. (1978). *Anna Karenina* (R.
   Edmonds, Trans.). Middlesex, England:
   Penguin. (Original work published 1878)

8. Work in an anthology

   Rogers, A. G. (1991). A feminist poetics of psychotherapy. In C. Gilligan, A. G. Rogers, &
   D. L. Tolman (Eds.), *Women, girls, and psychotherapy* (pp. 33-53). New York: Haworth
   Press.

9. Multivolume work

   Freedle, R. O. (Ed.). (1982). *Advances in
   discourse processes* (Vols. 1-9). Norwood,
   NJ: Ablex.

10. One volume from a multivolume work

    Tannen, D. (Ed.). (1982) *Spoken and written lan-
    guage: Exploring orality and literacy* (Vol. 9).
    Norwood, NJ: Ablex.

Periodicals

11. Article in a magazine

    Peterson, I. (1997, August 2). Silicon champions
    of the game. *Science News, 152,* 76-78.

12. Article in a journal (paginated by issue)

Salvner, G. M. (1995). The compass point.
English Journal, 84(4), 58-59.

13. Article in a journal (paginated by volume)

Bloom, L. Z. (1997). Why I (used to) hate
to give grades. *College Composition and
Communication, 48,* 360-371.

14. Unsigned article

Aluminum emerges as early timekeeper. (1996,
August 24). *Science News, 150,* 123.

15. Newspaper article
(Signed)

Greene, B. (1991, December 24). What's bad for
General Motors . . . . *Chicago Tribune,* p. 1.

(Unsigned)

Are interest-rate cuts any match for this recession?
(1991, December 23). *New York Times,* p. 5.

16. Magazine articles with no volume number
(Signed)

Diamond, J. (1989, June). The ethnobiologist's
dilemma. *Natural History Journal,* pp. 26, 28,
30.

(Unsigned)

Earthbound telescopes take on Hubble. (1991,
November). *Scientific American,* p. 121.

17. Review

Castro, E. (1997). [Review of the book *Maya's
children*]. *The Council Chronicle, 7*(1), 17.

Other sources

18. Electronic data file or database

National Council of Teachers of English. (1987).
On writing centers [Electronic data tape]. Urbana: ERIC Clearinghouse for Resolutions

on the Teaching of Composition, II. Silver-
Platter [Producer].

19. Unpublished dissertation listed in abstracts

Brozick, J. R. (1977). An investigation into the
composing process of four twelfth-grade students: Case studies based on Jung's personality
types, Freudian psychoanalytic ego psychology, and cognitive functioning. *Dissertation
Abstracts International, 38,* 31A-32A.

20. CD-ROM

Carnival. (1992). In *The Oxford English Dictionary*
[CD-ROM]. Oxford: Oxford Universtiy
Press.

21. Online journal

Fulghum, H. (1997, October). Gone into the
deep [6 paragraphs]. *Discovery Online:
Exploration* [on-line serial]. Available:
www.discovery.com/area/gone/gone.html.

22. Proceedings of a conference

Warnick, B. (1997). Masculinizing the feminine:
Inviting women online ca. 1997. In C. Glenn
& L. Ede (Eds.), *Proceedings of Feminism(s) &
Rhetoric(s): From Boundaries to Borderlands*
(pp. 25-37). Corvallis, OR: Oregon State
University Press.

23. Computer program

Deep Blue [Computer software]. (1997).
Yorktown, NY: IBM.

24. Government document

Office of the President of the United States
(1995). *Budget of the United States
Government: Fiscal Year.* Washington, DC:
U.S. Government Printing Office.

APA Manuscript Format

Materials, margins, spacing, indentation

Most computers and printers work with standard 8 1/2" × 11" paper, standard typefaces, and one-inch margins. Double-space unless asked to do otherwise, and indent paragraphs and quotations five spaces. Avoid odd typefaces or other unusual variations available for word processing. You're usually safe if you avoid anything that looks cute.

Page numbers and short title

Place page numbers in the upper right-hand corner, one-half inch from the top with a short title before (one or two words of the title will do).

Title page

Unless you're explicitly told not to, use one. Some instructors ask for title pages, and some just expect them. Journals ask for cover pages to detach for anonymity.

Punctuation and typing

Typesetting now calls for single spaces between sentences, but convention in nonprint texts still allows for two spaces (some instructors may prefer to read a text spaced this way). An em dash is formed by two hyphens with no space before, after, or between. On the computer, insert an em dash symbol.

References

Alphabetize the reference entries, indenting authors' names and initials.

Chicago

Chicago is the old-fashioned grandparent of citation styles. In addition to the picky differences between MLA and APA, you may encounter differences among various organizations and publishers, each of which uses its own style. Many styles refer to *The Chicago Manual of Style* when in doubt about a particular issue.

Chicago style resembles MLA style except that it

- cites sources in endnotes.
- lists sources alphabetically in a bibliography.
- uses fewer abbreviations than MLA.

Some professors, particularly in history, ask for endnotes rather than in-text citations. Endnotes are double-spaced, and the first line of each entry is indented five spaces. A bibliography is often required as well.

First reference to a source
The first note will include all publication information, which will also appear in a bibliography. The following notations demonstrate this format.

Endnotes

Books

1. Basic format for a book

    1. Lester Faigley, *Fragments of Rationality* (Pittsburgh: University of Pittsburgh Press, 1992), 61.

2. Two or three authors

    2. Maurice Scharton and Janice Neuleib, *Inside/Out: A Guide to Writing* (Boston: Allyn & Bacon, 1993), 33.

3. Four or more authors

    3. Sherman Manly et al., *Specimens of Pre-Shakespearean Drama* (London: Dover Press, 1960), 45.

4. Unknown author

    4. *Amphion Anglicus* (London: Norman Alternative Press, 1700), 23.

5. Author's name in title

    5. *The Complete Poems of Browning* (Boston: Houghton Mifflin, 1895), 1.

6. Edited work with an author

    6. Sherwood Anderson, *Tar: A Midwest Childhood,* ed. Ray Lewis White (Cleveland: Case Western Reserve University Press, 1969), 125.

7. Edited work without an author

>   7. C. S. Lewis, ed., *Essays Presented to Charles Williams* (Grand Rapids, Mich.: Eerdmans, 1966), ix.

8. Translated work

>   8. Franz Kafka, *The Castle,* trans. Willa Muir and Edwin Muir (London: Penguin, 1957), 109.

9. Revised edition

>   9. Joe Stuessy, *Rock and Roll: Its History and Stylistic Development,* 2d ed. (Englewood Cliffs, N.J.: Prentice-Hall, 1994), 47.

10. Biblical reference

>   10. Rom. 8:38 King James Version.

11. Work in an anthology

>   11. J. R. R. Tolkien, "On Fairy Stories," in *Essays Presented to Charles Williams,* ed. C. S. Lewis (Grand Rapids, Mich.: Eerdmans, 1966), 38.

12. Preface or introduction

>   12. Christopher Tolkien, introduction to *Unfinished Tales of Numenor and Middle-Earth,* by J. R. R. Tolkien, ed. Christopher Tolkien (Boston: Houghton Mifflin, 1980), 3.

13. Encyclopedia or dictionary

>   13. Eric Blom, ed., *Grove's Dictionary of Music and Musicians,* 5th ed., vol. 10, s.v. "cadence."

[s.v., or *sub verbo,* means "under the word"]

Periodicals

14. Newspaper article

>   14. Ann M. Job, "'98 Mazda 626 Pushes Right Buttons," *Pantagraph,* 2 November 1997, sec. D.

15. Article in a magazine with no volume number

    15. Jeffrey Goldsmith, "The Last Human Chessmaster," *Wired,* February 1995, 120.

16. Article in a periodical with continuous page numbering

    16. Lester Faigley, "Literacy after the Revolution," *College Composition and Communication* 48 (February 1997): 30.

17. Article in a periodical with each issue paged separately

    17. Marian M. Mohr, "Teacher-Researcher at Work," *English Journal* 83, no. 6 (1994): 20.

18. Review

    18. Gregory Clark, review of *Revisioning Writer's Talk: Gender and Culture in the Act of Composing,* by Mary Ann Cain, *College Composition and Communication* 48 (1997): 418.

Electronic and other sources

19. Information service

    19. Gene H. Brody and Zolinda Stoneman, "A Risk-Amelioration Model of Sibling Relationships: Conceptual Underpinnings and Preliminary Findings," *Advances in Applied Developmental Psychology* 10 (1996): 231-47 OVID, ERIC, ED 400989.

20. Online database

    20. Herman Haug. "Visiting Commemorative Places of the Mozart Family in Swabia, Germany" [German], *Acta Mozartiana* 43 (June 1996): 3-13, in OVID search [database online] (Urbana, Ill.: University of Illinois, 1997 [cited 10 March 1998]), available from <ovid/ .aiss.uic.edu/ibis/ovidweb/ovidweb.cgi?T.>)

21. Electronic journal or bulletin board

    21. Kim Heffner. "Bill Gates' Night Before Christmas" [electronic bulletin board], 10 November 1997 [cited 20 December 1997]. Available from 0_882562640@inet_out.mail.aol.com.3.

22. Computer software

    22. BodyWorks 4.0, The Learning Company Inc., Cambridge, Mass.

23. Unpublished dissertation

    23. Claire Lamonica, "Conflict and Creativity in Student Writing Groups" (Ph.D. diss., Illinois State University, 1996), 187.

24. Anonymous pamphlet

    24. *Aaron Copland: A Catalogue of His Works* (New York: Boosey & Hawks, n.d.).

25. A letter in a published collection

    25. C. S. Lewis to Arthur Greeves, 10 October 1943, *Letters of C. S. Lewis to Arthur Greeves,* ed. Walter Hooper. (New York: Macmillan, 1979), 23.

26. An unpublished or personal letter

    26. C. S. Lewis, letter to an anonymous lady, 4 June 1941, Lewis Archives, Wheaton College, Wheaton, Ill.

27. Personal or telephone interview

    27. Marian Palm, interview by author, Roseburg, Oregon, 1 September 1997.

28. Videocassette

    28. *Star Wars,* prod. and dir. Steven Spielberg, 3 hr. 12 min., Warner, 1978, videocassette.

29. Record, tape, or CD

    29. John Whelan, *Celtic Reflections,* Narada compact disk ND-61052.

30. Source quoted in another source

      30. Clifford Geertz, *The Interpretation of Cultures* (New York: Basic Books, 1973), 360, quoted in Karen Burke LeFevre, *Invention as a Social Act* (Carbondale: Southern Illinois University Press, 1987), 119.

Subsequent reference to a source
In most cases, simply give the author's last name and a page number if available.

      31. Faigley, 23.

When citing an author more than once, use a short form of the title in addition to the name.

      32. Sommers, *Life in Time,* 23.

      33. Sommers, "Girls Back Then," 14.

"Ibid." may be used for repeated sources. Note that "op. cit." and "loc. cit." are no longer used.

Bibliography

Books

1. Basic format for a book
   Faigley, Lester. *Fragments of Rationality.* Pittsburgh: University of Pittsburgh Press, 1992.

2. Two or three authors
   Scharton, Maurice, and Janice Neuleib. *Inside/Out: A Guide to Writing.* Boston: Allyn & Bacon, 1993.

3. Four or more authors
   Manly, Sherman, et al. *Specimens of Pre-Shakespearean Drama.* London: Dover Press, 1960.

4. Unknown author
   Amphion Anglicus. London: Norman Alternative Press, 1700.

5. Author's name in title

Browning, Robert. *The Complete Poems of Browning.* Boston: Houghton Mifflin, 1895.

6. Edited work with an author

Anderson, Sherwood. *Tar: A Midwest Childhood.* Edited by Ray Lewis White. Cleveland: Case Western Reserve University Press, 1969.

7. Edited work without an author

Lewis, C. S., ed. *Essays Presented to Charles Williams.* Grand Rapids, Mich.: Eerdmans, 1966.

8. Translated work

Kafka, Franz. *The Castle.* Translated by Willa and Edwin Muir. London: Penguin, 1957.

9. Revised edition

Stuessy, Joe. *Rock and Roll: Its History and Stylistic Development.* 2d ed. Englewood Cliffs, NJ: Prentice-Hall, 1994.

10. Biblical reference

Bibles are not generally listed in the bibliography.

11. Work in an anthology

Tolkien, J. R. R. "On Fairy Stories." In *Essays Presented to Charles Williams,* edited by C. S. Lewis, 38-49. Grand Rapids, Mich.: Eerdmans, 1966.

12. Preface or introduction

Tolkien, Christopher. Introduction to *Unfinished Tales of Numenor and Middle-Earth,* by J. R. R. Tolkien, edited by Christopher Tolkien. Boston: Houghton Mifflin, 1980.

13. Encyclopedia or dictionary

Well-known reference books such as encyclopedias and dictionaries are not generally listed in the bibliography.

Periodicals

14. Newspaper article

Job, Ann M. "'98 Mazda 626 Pushes Right
Buttons." *Pantagraph,* 2 November 1997,
sec. D.

15. Article in a magazine with no volume number

Goldsmith, Jeffrey. "The Last Human
Chessmaster." *Wired,* February 1995, 120-24.

16. Article in a periodical with continuous page numbering

Faigley, Lester. "Literacy after the Revolution."
College Composition and Communication 48
(February 1997): 30-57.

17. Article in a periodical with each issue paged separately

Mohr, Marian M. "Teacher-Researcher at Work."
English Journal 83, no. 6 (1994): 20-24.

18. Review

Clark, Gregory. Review of *Revisioning Writer's Talk:
Gender and Culture in the Act of Composing,* by
Mary Ann Cain. *College Composition and
Communication* 48 (1997): 418.

Electronic and other sources

19. Information service

Brody, Gene H., and Zolinda Stoneman. "A Risk-
Amelioration Model of Sibling Relation-
ships: Conceptual Underpinnings and Pre-
liminary Findings." *Advances in Applied
Developmental Psychology* 10 (1996): 231-47.
OVID, ERIC, ED 400989.

20. Online database

Haug, Herman. "Visiting Commemorative Places
of the Mozart Family in Swabia, Germany"

[German]. *Acta Mozartiana* 43 (June 1996): 3-13. In OVID search [database online]. Urbana, Ill.: University of Illinois, 1997. [cited 10 March 1998]. Available from <ovid/ .aiss.uic.edu/ibis/ovidweb/ovidweb.cgi?T.>

21. Electronic journal or bulletin board
    Heffner, Kim. "Bill Gates' Night Before Christmas" [electronic bulletin board], 10 November 1997 [cited 20 December 1997]. Available from 0_882562640@inet_out.mail.aol.com.3.

22. Computer software
    BodyWorks 4.0. The Learning Company Inc., Cambridge, Mass.

23. Unpublished dissertation
    Lamonica, Claire. "Conflict and Creativity in Student Writing Groups." Ph.D. diss., Illinois State University, 1996.

24. Anonymous pamphlet
    Aaron Copland: A Catalogue of His Works. New York: Boosey & Hawks, n.d.

25. A letter in a published collection
    Lewis, C. S. *Letters of C. S. Lewis to Arthur Greeves.* Edited by Walter Hooper. New York: Macmillan, 1979.

26. An unpublished or personal letter
    Lewis, C. S. Letter to an anonymous lady. 4 June 1941. Lewis Archives, Wheaton College, Wheaton, Ill.

Note: Only archived personal communications are included in bibliographies; other personal communications do not appear in bibliographies.

27. Personal or telephone interview
    Madden, Joanie. Interview by Maria Liasson. Public Broadcasting System. 1 September 1997.

28. Videocassette

> *Star Wars*. Produced and directed by Steven
> Spielberg. 3 hr. 12 min. Warner, 1978.
> Videocassette.

29. Record, tape, or CD

> Whelan, John. *Celtic Reflections*. Narada compact
> disk ND-61052.

30. Source quoted in another source

> Geertz, Clifford. *The Interpretation of Cultures,* 360.
> New York: Basic Books, 1973. Quoted in
> Karen Burke LeFevre, *Invention as a Social
> Act* (Carbondale: Southern Illinois Univer-
> sity Press, 1987), 119.

Chicago Manuscript Format

Title and identification
The title page includes name and course number or
address for material submitted for publication. No
page number appears on the title page.

Margins and spacing
Margins should be at least one inch on all sides. All
parts of the text should be double-spaced, including
block quotations.

Pagination
Page numbers appear in the upper right-hand corner. A name or short title may be added as required
by an instructor or the publisher.

Notes
Number notes pages consecutively with the text of
the paper. Number notes with arabic numerals, followed by a period and a space. Double-space notes.
Authors' names are not inverted in notes. Use *and*
for two or three authors, and *et al.* for more than four
authors. Do not use *p.* or *pp.*

Bibliography
This page generally follows the notes. The items are
alphabetized by the last name of the author or, where

no author is available, by the first major word in the title (omitting *a, an,* and *the* for purposes of alphabetization).

Research

Though not all papers are research papers, many academic papers require some research. When using information or ideas from another source, you need to select information carefully, cite intelligently and thoughtfully (avoiding plagiarism), and integrate the researched information skillfully into your own arguments.

Supporting a Thesis

Not all papers state a thesis exactly, but all papers do present a thesis, either in so many words or indirectly in the arguments of the text. When beginning to write a paper, you should start with a working thesis to help focus the work. The thesis works in the same way as a house plan does. If you lay out the design for a new house on a computer program, you first have to choose the basic design for the house: two stories or one, three bedrooms or four, two-car garage or three-, and so on. A thesis resembles the builder's basic plans for certain designs. You can keep changing the design until the actual walls go up, or in the case of a paper, until it has been turned in for the final time.

The work usually follows a pattern that includes a set of questions. In the following essay on IBM's Deep Blue, the writer might have posed an original question, something like "Do machines really express human ingenuity, and is Deep Blue an example of the human creative impulse?" The writer then began to read newspaper articles, web sites, and information from the chess tournament itself. As he read, he narrowed and refined the question into this thesis:

> Kasparov's defeat signified a victory for the human race because, if anyone represented us in the chess match, it was not the chess genius who struggled in isolation to defeat all challengers, but the humans who created Deep Blue.

The thesis remains a subject of debate, but the essay strives to prove the writer's point.

Notice again the order of the work:

1. Develop research questions.
2. Read to expand and then narrow the topic.
3. Develop a working thesis.

Organizing Ideas and Sources

This part of the writing can be challenging because the writing may have begun with brainstorming or drafting as the materials were being gathered. Finally, there will be a mixture of your own ideas and arguments and of the materials gathered. The problem will be to sort out all the parts to produce a readable and original essay.

The easiest first step is to list the key points that will likely appear in the paper. In the case of the Deep Blue paper, these are

1. The *New York Times* argued that Deep Blue defeated humanity.
2. Machines have already defeated humanity in strength and speed.
3. Deep Blue did beat Kasparov.
4. The machine was clearly a product of its chip designers and program writers.
5. Humanity achieved a great technological leap.

The paper itself builds on these points, using the following topic sentences to make each of the points that the paragraphs will develop.

1. According to the *Times* writer, it was "a decisive weekend for chess, and humanity" (Weber, D23).
2. Kasparov had not dropped dead, but his ego had been devastated by science and technology, twin monsters that feed insatiably on knowledge and problems.
3. In fact, the human race went on about its business.
4. Kasparov's defeat signified a victory for the human race because, if anyone represented us in the chess match, it was not the chess genius who

struggled in isolation to defeat all challengers, but the humans who created Deep Blue. (This topic sentence is also the thesis sentence.)

5. Knowing how Deep Blue defeated Kasparov, we should balance our human fear that "that hammer's gonna be the death of me" with gratitude for the knowledge that science and technology immeasurably lengthen the human life span, directly through the medicines that improve human health and indirectly through the machines that multiply the work we can accomplish, the distances we can travel, and the information we can command.

The author also could have listed general research questions to help him clarify his investigation.

1. What did the news say about the chess match?
2. What kind of machine was the computer?
3. What kinds of discovery and programming went into the computer?
4. What does the chess defeat really mean?

These questions would have focused both the research and the writing. In the case of this essay, the writer had access to the chess match program but needed to find other information from the news and the Internet to build and support his arguments.

Supporting Each Point

Each of the points in the paper was expanded to explain the writer's argument.

1. *The* New York Times *argued that Deep Blue defeated humanity.* The author explained the *Times*'s position and compared Kasparov's defeat to John Henry's being beaten by a steam hammer.
2. *Machines have already defeated humanity in strength and speed.* The author elaborates this point to show Kasparov's distress and his apparent joining of other humans who have bowed to machines.
3. *Deep Blue did beat Kasparov.* The author expands this point by showing that only Kasparov's ego

was beaten. The machine itself was a triumph for other humans.

4. *The machine was clearly a product of its chip designers and program writers.* Here, the author uses his research to explain the work that went into the machine and its great testimony to human abilities.

5. *Humanity achieved a great technological leap.* The author ends by showing that the machine has many applications and that Kasparov himself lives on as the intellectual model for the parallel processors' approach to chess.

Sample Paper MLA

Deep Blue and the Ghost of John Henry

"This hammer's gonna be the death of me, lawd, lawd."

—The Ballad of John Henry

On Saturday, May 10, 1997, the *New York Times* ran a story on the chess match between Deep Blue, IBM's supercomputer, and Garry Kasparov, the world's greatest human chess player. According to the *Times* writer, it was "a decisive weekend for chess, and humanity" (Weber D23). If Deep Blue prevailed, then machines would have proved themselves smarter than people. Since machines had already proved themselves stronger than people, what except the soul would be left to feed the ego's need to believe in its innate and individual superiority? The *Times* writer played on his readers' fears of science and technology in a way that recalled the nineteenth-century ballad "John Henry." According to the ballad, the steel-driving railroad worker, John Henry, dropped dead trying to drive railroad spikes faster than a steam hammer designed to do the same job. John Henry's ghost has haunted the imagination of twentieth-century humanity as a fear that our inventions may eventually destroy us.

On Sunday, May 11, 1997, only nineteen moves and less than an hour into the sixth game of the match (*Inside Chess,* para. 1), Garry Kasparov extended his hand to Joe Hoane, Deep Blue's programmer, in a gesture of resignation: the computer had won game and match (Peterson 76). Kasparov had not dropped dead, but his ego had been devastated by science and technology, twin monsters that feed insatiably on knowledge and problems. Now that a machine had defeated the world's best human competitor at a game many considered the ultimate test of human intelligence, had humanity's place in the world changed?

According to the *Times,* Kasparov was "holding the human race on his shoulders" (Weber D23). To the *Times,* Kasparov's defeat implied that humankind had tumbled off Kasparov's shoulders and landed ignominiously at Deep Blue's feet (if a machine that looks like two filing cabinets can be said to have feet). In fact, the human race went on about its business. Kasparov and his grandmaster cronies continued to fiddle with their chess pieces, no more superfluous than they ever were. Even Kasparov's ego almost surely regenerated itself using the knowledge that winning the match did not make Deep Blue a grandmaster any more than circling Kitty Hawk made the Wright brothers' airplane a seagull. Finally, nothing important was lost that weekend, and a great victory for the human race was gained.

Kasparov's defeat signified a victory for the human race because, if anyone represented us in the chess match, it was not the chess genius who struggled in isolation to defeat all challengers, but the humans who created Deep Blue. Like the dreamers who studied birds to understand their gift of flight, Deep Blue's designers modeled their strategy on generations of human chessmaster games. Like the inventors of powered flight, Deep Blue's engineers modified the available technology of their generation of scientists to create thirty-two "Super Chip (P2SC) nodes" and thereby to attain the superhuman analytical speed of two hundred million board positions per second (Newborn 7). In challenging Kasparov, Deep Blue's inventors stood on the shoulders of the generations of chessmasters, scientists, and engineers who preceded them. Future generations of scientists will transcend Deep Blue's technology to reach toward solutions to meteorological, economic, medical, engineering, and mathematical problems important to the whole human race. Meanwhile, new generations of families will gather around retired Deep Blues for schoolwork, video games, and Internet amusements.

Knowing how Deep Blue defeated Kasparov, we should balance our human fear that "that hammer's gonna be the death of me" with gratitude for the knowledge that science and technology immeasurably lengthen the human life span, directly through the medicines that improve human health and indirectly through the machines that multiply the work we can accomplish, the distances we can travel, and the information we can command. Finally, we should consider this. Deep Blue's thirty-two parallel processors were designed to divide and conquer the complex problems of the chessboard at unimaginable speed, with the sole purpose of beating Garry Kasparov. Thus, Kasparov's mind lives on in the electronic synapses of the machine created to defeat him, as John Henry's ghost lingers in the steel sinews of the machines that perform his job. No one could ask for a nobler monument.

Works Cited

"Inside Chess Online." 4 Apr. 1997 <www.grandmaster.bc.ca/chess/kasparov.html>.

Newborn, Monty, and George Paul, eds. *Kasparov vs. Deep Blue: The Rematch.* Program of ACM Society Conference. New York. 3-11 May 1997.

Peterson, Ivars. "Silicon Champions of the Game." *Science News* 152 (1997): 76-78.

Weber, Bruce. "The Contest Is Toe-to-Toe and Pawn-to-Pawn." *New York Times* 10 May 1997: D21+.

Sample Paper APA

True Science or Why Men?

Grace Witherspoon

Illinois State University

Noted humorist, Dave Barry, reports a scientific study conducted by two Canadian psychologists. These psychologists wished to investigate the differences in male and female responses to humor. To determine these differences, they exposed both genders to *Three Stooges* clips and to Hugh Grant movies. The guys all preferred *The Three Stooges* whereas the women all smiled warmly at Hugh Grant movies. Barry notes that the scientists concluded that *The Three Stooges* appeal to two groups: "1. People with brain damage, and 2. Men" (Barry, March 2000). The women studied in the project all preferred Hugh Grant videos. Barry often reports such scientific studies for his readers, offering vital information to those interested in wacky science. He also provides his own reasoned explanations of current social, historical, and political issues that relate to science. In an essay on oil and dinosaurs, he attempts to explain the economics and mathematics of gasoline prices by returning the reader to the "Voracious Period" when dinosaurs roamed the earth eating everything in their paths, "except for broccoli, which they hated" (Barry, April 2000). After a careful explanation of the dinosaurs' tragic end (a comet killed them all at once, thus producing tons of oil and leading to Middle East conflicts) Barry concludes that the only scientific solution to the current oil crisis is to create more dinosaurs to kill and crush into oil. Barry's logic is good; his science is a trifle fuzzy.

Though scientists usually are about as funny as accountants and passport control officers, real scientific investigations can often be as funny as Barry's pseudo-science. In fact, the results of most scientific studies often seem intended to amuse. In an experiment reported recently in *Psychology Today*, researchers at Williams, Cornell, and Northwestern universities, sent "a student wearing a Barry Manilow T-shirt" into a room filled with peers (Rooney, p. 20). In the results of this experiment, fewer than half the students in the room recalled the T-shirt. The study fails to note how many of those students who did notice the shirt mercilessly ridiculed those bearing Manilow on their chests.

This study was supposed to show that we notice ourselves more than others notice us. In fact, the research shows the bizarre cruelty of the researchers.
What worse humiliation could be inflicted on a
young person than to ask him or her to wear a Barry
Manilow T-shirt in the name of science?

This kind of malice appears in the natural envi-
ronment as well as in the planning labs of scientific
researchers. In *Why Things Bite Back*, Edward Tenner,
whimsical Princeton physics professor, explains that
for every good outcome of human invention or natural "evolution" there will be a confounding negative response. Just one story illustrates the horrors
of nature's revenges. A secretary of the U.S. Commission of Fish and Fisheries decided to solve the problem of a decrease in the number of American lake
fish by introducing German carp into American
lakes. National carp ponds were established "at the
foot of the Washington Monument" (p. 165). Soon
police officers were called in to protect young carp
from national Fourth of July fireworks. Citizens began requesting carp "through their congressmen" by
mail. It was soon found that carp grow lazy and taste
foul if not exercised. Soon methods were being developed to exercise carp, including introducing pike
whose presence increased carp athletics, since "recent research shows that carp can bulk up defen-
sively in the presence of pike" (p. 165). The reader
is left with the image of carp lifting weights and
building truly puffy pecs to face a school of menac-
ing pike.

While carp grow stronger, pigs are preparing to
give their lives for humans and not just for breakfast
anymore. Researchers in England have developed a
strain of pigs that can be used in human transplants.

Formerly, human bodies rejected animal organs, but scientists have planted human genes in pigs and produced pigs with organs that can be used in humans. So the investigators say that they are working toward "an unlimited supply of compatible pig organs for human transplantation" (Polejaeva, 2000). Does this mean that more and more humans will be making oinking noises and preferring mud baths to Jacuzzis?

Perhaps all those porcine humans will all be females, too. In *The Red Queen: Sex and the Evolution of Human Nature*, Matt Ridley explains why nature seems eager to make redundant the male of nearly every species (probably because guys insist on watching *The Three Stooges* rather than thinking about the next generation). Eggs from turkeys vaccinated for foul pox tended to develop into unfertilized turkey embryos. By using these live viruses, scientists produced a strain of turkeys "nearly half of whose eggs would begin to develop without sperm" (p. 109). The potential for this research seems obvious. Guys could watch *The Three Stooges;* girls could get their chicken pox vaccinations; babies would appear spontaneously so that guys would never have to leave the TV set. The whole problem of the battle between the sexes would be solved. A race of superwomen could evolve, and eventually all *Three Stooges* tapes could become landfill. Science has shown the way.

References

Barry, D. (2000, March 19). Three Stooges from Mars, Hugh Grant is from Venus. *The Pantagraph,* p. B1.

_____. (2000, April 16). We're just a few dinosaurs short of a full tank of gas. *The Pantagraph,* p. B1.

Hessel, R. (1875-1876). The carp and its culture in rivers and lakes: and its introduction in America. In U.S. Commission of Fish and Fisheries, Part IV, pp. 865-97. Rpt. in Tenner, E. (1997). *Why things bite back.* New York: Random House.

Olsen, M. W., & Marsden, S. J. (1954). Natural parthenogenesis of turkey eggs. *Science, 120*(3), 545-546.

Polejeava, I. A., Chen, S., Vaught, T. D., Page, R. L., Mullins, J., Ball, S., Dai, Y., Boone, J., Walker, S., Ayares, D. L., Colman, A., & Campbell, K. H. S. (2000). Cloned pigs produced by nuclear transfer from adult somatic cells. *Nature, 407,* 86-90 [on-line serial]. Available FTP: <www.nature.com/cgitaf/ DynaPage.taf?file=/ nature/journal/v407/n6800/full/ 407086a0_fs.html>

Ridley, M. (1993). *The red queen: Sex and the evolution of human nature.* New York: Penguin.

Rooney, M. (1998, October). In the spotlight. *Psychology Today,* 20.

| COMPUTER TIP |

Use the computer to manage large documents.

1. Name your documents logically.
   The cute and casual name you invent on the spur of the moment might not make any sense to you in a week when you look for the document again. Develop a system for naming all your documents. If you have two courses you're writing papers for, use your last name, the course number, the assignment and draft numbers for each document. The second draft of my first English 101 paper might be named scharton.101.1.2. You'll find the docu-

ments line up magically in an easy order on your disk or hard drive.

2. Save documents in Rich Text Format.

Form the habit of saving documents in Rich Text Format (RTF). You'll find this option in a dialog box if you use "save as" to save your document. RTF files move successfully from one computer program to another. You're not so likely to find the Martian gobbledygook when you open a file at home that you created in the lab at school.

3. Move your mouse to left margin to select a line, a paragraph, or the whole text.

At the left margin, one click will select a line, a double-click will select the paragraph, and a triple-click will select the whole document.

4. Use the track changes feature of your word processing program to compare drafts.

To inform yourself about the changes between drafts of a paper, open the latest draft, go to track changes, and select the compare documents function. The differences will appear highlighted in your present text. Noting the differences can help you to see the progress of your thinking. Your instructor may ask you to describe the reasons for your changes in a cover letter for the research paper or for your portfolio.

5. Use e-mail attachments to transfer documents from person to person and place to place.

You can save yourself the trouble of carrying around floppy disks if you learn to attach documents to e-mail messages. While working at home, you can send a document to yourself and pick it up at your computer lab. You can send a copy to a teacher or collaborator for comments. If you forget your disk, you can send a document to yourself at home. To avoid trouble opening attachments, it's a good practice to attach the document and also copy and paste it into the text of the e-mail message.

6. Use track changes to do collaborative work.

When you read someone else's writing, locate and turn on the track changes function. Check the highlight changes option. Your comments or changes will appear in a different color, and the original text will remain, allowing the author to work through your changes one at a time, accepting or rejecting them.

7. Use the outline view for large-scale reorganization.
   In outline view, the size of your text is reduced, so that you can see more of it. You can easily select a paragraph or series of paragraphs and use the up and down arrows in outline view to move the text wherever you want it to go.

8. Use outline view to check for format.
   Use the outline view to check your final draft for consistency of typeface, headings, and spacing. To get an overview of your document, select the outline view, which suppresses all but the first line of each paragraph.

9. Use outline view to make a table of contents for your research paper.
   Use the outline view to provide subheads for long documents such as research papers. Not only will they make the document easier to read, the computer can use the outline heads to automatically generate a table of contents. Better still, you can revise the document, rerun the table of contents function, and a new updated table of contents appears.

10. Put your title page in a separate section.
    Keeping your title page separate from your main document will cut down on confusion in page numbering. Insert a section break after the title page, and specify that page numbering begin with 1 in the new section.

Citing Sources and Avoiding Plagiarism

When referring to another's work or ideas, you should use brief direct quotes to show a point that is important. Note how the Deep Blue author uses the exact words of the newspaper to stress the excitement of the chess match. When not quoting directly, read the material, then put it aside and integrate the information in your own words and ideas. You still must refer to the source (note the reference to the program listed under Newborn in the sample paper's Works Cited list), but the words and the arguments will be your own.

Consistent system for citation

You must cite a source when you quote words or when you refer to an argument, statistic, or idea. The various disciplines use their own forms of citation (see documentation for MLA, APA, and *Chicago Manual of Style*). Certain rules apply in all cases.

1. The author is named either in the text introducing the material or in a parenthetical citation.
2. The reference is followed by the page number in parentheses.
3. A list of works cited appears at the end of the paper, listed alphabetically. Chicago style also lists notes.

Sample in-text citation

According to the *Times*, Kasparov was "holding the human race on his shoulders" (Weber D23).

Sample entry in Works Cited

Weber, Bruce. "The Contest Is Toe-to-Toe and Pawn-to-Pawn." *New York Times*. 10 May 1997: D21+.

Avoiding plagiarism

As you begin researching your paper, your teacher and classmates will help you to develop your work. At this point, they will note any misuse of outside materials. Later on in your academic work, you will have to learn to guard yourself carefully as you work.

Legally, plagiarism is defined as:

1. lack of citation of either direct wording or ideas,
2. using direct wording without quotation marks, and
3. using some of the author's wording in summaries or paraphrases.

Citing quotations

Any words that come from another text must be cited. An exception is common knowledge, such as that the earth and planets circle the sun or that Shakespeare wrote during the Renaissance. As you read through sources, when an idea appears more than once and is not cited, you may consider it common knowledge in the field. When in doubt about what is common knowledge from a source, it is best to cite.

Quotation marks must be used around all cited materials.

> According to the *Times* writer, it was "a decisive weekend for chess, and humanity" (Weber D23).

The paraphrase must be in your own words.

> On Sunday, May 11, 1997, only nineteen moves and less than an hour into the sixth game of the match (Inside Chess para. 1), Garry Kasparov extended his hand to Joe Hoane, Deep Blue's programmer, in a gesture of resignation: the computer had won game and match (Peterson 76).

The original source gives a detailed account of the history and events of the match; this sentence paraphrases several paragraphs of the article.

Quotations integrated into the text

Even mature writers sometimes pay too little attention to inserting quotations. They must be introduced and carefully worked into the meaning of the text. It is best if they add something that the text itself could not have said as well.

> According to the *Times*, Kasparov was "holding the human race on his shoulders" (Weber D23).

The *Times* writer uses a specific image that catches the mood of the match.

Always choose wording that clearly connects the cited quotation with your own writing. Words such as *admits, contends, notes, thinks,* or *points out* work well if they fit with the passage. Note that the quote above is blended into the text of the essay by the use of the phrase "according to the *Times*." Also note that only part of a sentence is worked into the text. Usually, the less quoted the better. Use only the best words and paraphrase the rest.

The ellipsis mark and brackets
The ellipsis   To keep quoted materials short, use the ellipsis (...) to cut out pieces of long quotations. Choose only the most important parts of the quote.

> "he was . . . holding the human race on his shoulders"

Brackets   Use brackets to insert your own words into the quoted materials.

> "holding [like Hercules] the human race on his shoulders"

The writer of the paper could have inserted the bracketed phrase to explain the allusion.

Setting off long quotations
Good writing usually avoids long quotations, especially for reasonably short papers. If you must use long quotations, indent the quotation and omit the marks. (See MLA and APA sections for specific guidelines.)

Quoting a source quoted in another source
When quoting a source from another source, use a signal phrase referring to the original source and follow the citation with (qtd. in *Name*).

Integrating other sources
Sources include not only summaries but also statistics and other kinds of data.

Paraphrases and summaries   These are simply combined in the text with careful citation of the source.

> On Saturday, May 10, 1997, the *New York Times* ran a story in which reporter Weber commented on the chess match between Deep Blue, IBM's supercomputer, and Garry Kasparov, the world's greatest human chess player (D23).

The sentence quickly summarizes the details of the event, noting that reporter Weber provided the material.

Statistics and facts

On Saturday, May 10, 1997, the *New York Times* ran a story on the chess match between Deep Blue, IBM's supercomputer, and Garry Kasparov, the world's greatest human chess player (Weber D23).

Here, the date of the chess match is blended into the text. A signal phrase could also be used.

New York Times reporter Weber noted that on Saturday, May 10, 1997, a chess match took place between Deep Blue, IBM's supercomputer, and Garry Kasparov, the world's greatest human chess player (Weber D23).

General Advice on Manuscript Format

To review manuscript format, use your word-processing program's page preview or proof function. Pretend that the text is something that should be shaped attractively, a picture or a garden or a roomful of furniture. Within the requirements of the style (APA, MLA, Chicago) you must use, your goal should be to make each page look balanced and symmetrical. Work on one page till you like the way it looks, and follow through with that look on the rest of the pages. We've listed some important page features, along with suggested ways to handle them.

Page Layout

Typeface must treat the reader's eye gently, above all. If you can choose from a number of typefaces on your computer, work with a twelve-point face that has serifs, those little feet at the bottom of the letters, like the typeface in this book. Resist the temptation to play with typefaces. You want readers thinking about your ideas, not trying to decipher your code.

Indentation usually runs five spaces for new paragraphs (or 1/4" on the computer). You may need to use "hanging" indentation (the first line flush left, with the second and successive lines indented) for Works Cited pages. Your word-processing program can handle hanging indentation, and you'll look very smooth.

Spacing should be like your favorite grandparent: consistent and generous. Double-space within and between paragraphs. Add an extra space at the end of sections of your manuscript.

Margins should be consistent all around: usually an inch on the top and bottom and an inch and a quarter on the right and left will present an image that's easy on the eye.

Widows (i.e., the last lines of paragraphs that occur all by themselves at the top of a page) aren't allowed. You must move another line to the top of the page. Most word-processing programs have a way of handling widows automatically. Leaving the first line of a paragraph at the bottom of a page is not allowed, either. Move the line to the next page so it doesn't look like you were assassinated before you could finish the paragraph.

Page numbers should be placed in the upper right-hand corner of each page except the first one.

Headings operate just like outlines. Use headings to enable people to move around quickly in your manuscript, and ignore your explanations when they feel like it. Use spacing and typeface to signal different outline levels logically. For example, main headings might be centered, boldfaced, and capitalized; subheadings might move to the left margin ("flush left"), be boldfaced, and have only the first word capitalized ("sentence case").

Quotations should flow naturally into the rest of the text. A large block quotation is like putting out a loaf of unsliced bread and bologna for guests. Better to slice it up and serve it with some warmth or relish.

Lists should be indented more than regular text and bulleted if your audience allows it. As a general rule, bullets are expected by public, business, or technical audiences, but loathed by academic audiences.

COMPUTER TIP

If you are posting a piece of your writing on the Web, keep in mind a few design principles. This is your chance to do a better job than the people who designed the traffic patterns in your town.

1. Background color—Change the color from the nasty battleship gray that is default. Afterwards, check to be sure your text has not disappeared into the background. Choose and stay with a single background color for all your pages.

2. Background pattern—If you decide to use a patterned background, check to see what effects the background has on text readability. Choose and stay with a single background pattern for all your pages.

3. Dead links—Check your links to be sure they continue to work.

4. Navigation bars—You can speed use of your text with a simple table at the top of each page that includes links to all relevant pages.

5. Text in odd fonts, boldface, italics, colors, or all capitals—Avoid text treatments that are difficult to read.

6. "Under Construction" signs, flashing words, animated gifs, hit counters—This is a short list of features found on unprofessional Web sites; avoid them.

7. Wide, wide pages; long, long pages; huge, slow graphics—Web surfers will move the party down the beach if your pages are slow to load or navigate.

8. External links to other sites—Don't link to other people's sites or pages. They won't have return links to your page, and the foreign pages may change or disappear. If you find pages you just have to share, create a link library, and put it somewhere unobtrusive.

9. Linked text—Feel free to link your text to pages you have constructed rather than creating single pages that require scrolling. Remember to include a back function or a navigation bar that will speed users back to their point of origin.

6

A Little Grammar (Never Hurt Anyone)

Even kings must obey the laws of grammar.

(Jean-Baptiste Molière)

You've covered this material in at least eight years of public education, more if you went to parochial school. Before you go for repetition number nine, count the clauses in the extract below. Since many rules about sentence structure, word choice, and punctuation are based on the clause concept, writers need, as a practical matter, to be able to identify clauses in order to follow the rules.

A Little Grammar Test

Grammar and mythology operate the same way: they both provide a system of names that helps people to discuss and control the world of the mind. The people who created the classical pantheon of gods and goddesses were naming forces they perceived in the world and in themselves. External realities such as trees and rivers became nymphs and minor gods, while internal realities such as love and anger became more important deities, Venus and Mars. By naming external and internal realities, the authors of classical mythology gained the ability to think and talk about the world in familiar terms, which is a kind of control. Similar control is achieved when people use terms such as *noun* and *verb* to achieve a sense of control over the language they use. Coincidentally, classical mythology and grammar come to us from the same sources: Greek and Latin texts written before the Middle Ages. The same scholars who revived classical learning during the Renaissance used the Latin grammar they knew in order to write an English grammar: to discuss, analyze, and, they hoped, to control the development of English.

See Appendix 5 (p. 193) to score your test. If you found all eighteen clauses, just get back to work writing. You've demonstrated that you know enough grammar to handle sentence structure and punctuation. If you didn't locate all eighteen clauses, you may find it helpful to refer to this chapter occasionally to understand the grammatical concepts used in the other chapters, but don't expect miracles.

We have good news and bad news about grammar. First the good news: grammar provides a simple structure for naming the elements of English, like the chemist's periodic table of the elements. All the words in English can be classified into parts of speech. All the sentences in English can also be analyzed into parts. Using this elegant two-tier system, anyone can understand the structure of an infinite variety of statements about the world; talk about mental objects and events associated with language; and use familiar terms such as *noun* and *verb*, *sentence* and *phrase* to study style or to follow proofreading rules. The simple act of naming the parts of speech and the parts of sentences can give a writer a control over language that feels magical.

The bad news is that grammar also provides a landing point from which a rag-tag regiment of kooks, cranks, obsessive-compulsives, curmudgeonly professors, meddling bureaucrats, and self-appointed language cops can infiltrate and sabotage education all along its frontiers. Schedule a school board meeting on raising standards, ask a committee to plan a writing course, or announce a lecture on language anywhere, and the Lost Grammar Battalion suddenly emerges from the undergrowth wearing moss-covered combat gear from every war in the last three hundred years.

Militant grammarians believe, despite a conspicuous lack of factual evidence, that people learn to write by learning grammar. This belief stems from faulty thinking about cause and effect too complex to explain here (suffice it to say that the same pattern of thinking would support a belief that your nose grew in the middle of your face to provide a place to put your sunglasses). Militant grammarians are probably the main reason children must endure grammar drills ("Attention! Right shoulder, nouns!") every year starting in early elementary school. In turn, the teachers who must cover grammar at eleven or twelve grade levels have produced the assorted conflicting ways of "simplifying" grammar that afflict all of us and leave us feeling like taking a nap, or like throwing our grammar book at someone and then taking a nap.

If your school experiences with grammar have given you grammar anxiety, relax. When, as you contemplate concepts such as the conjunctive adverb or the passive voice, you feel a coma or a tantrum coming on, take a deep breath, let your mind drift to your happy place, and exhale slowly. Then read the explanation, absorbing as much as you can from one pass over the material, and get back to writing.

Parts of Speech

The phrase *parts of speech* denotes the set of labels given words in English. When you look up a word in the dictionary, you'll see its part-of-speech designation listed just after the pronunciation. There are eight parts of speech:

- nouns, pronouns, and adjectives;
- verbs and adverbs;
- prepositions and conjunctions;
- and interjections.

A single word can function as two or three different parts of speech; for example, the word *love* functions as a noun ("Be my love") or a verb ("I love you") or an adjective ("Marilyn Monroe was a movie love goddess").

Nouns

Noun means "name." Nouns give names to

- persons, places, and things, such as *Hannah, Greece,* and *candle;*
- abstractions, such as *love, belief,* and *goddess.*

Nouns can work in blends to name things as well, as in *truth-value* or *fairy tale*. Articles (*a, an,* and *the*) can help to identify nouns. Where you find an article, a noun will follow:

> I'm coming to *the party* in *a breech cloth* and feathered bonnet, as Kokapelli, *a playful character* in Native American mythology, who is pictured dancing and playing *the flute*.

Proper and common nouns
Nouns that must be capitalized (*Dorothy, Oz*) are called proper nouns. All others are called common nouns (*witch, country*). (See Capitalization, pp. 106–108.)

Singular, plural, and collective nouns
Nouns usually have singular or plural forms (*dragon, dragons*), though collective nouns may be either singular or plural (*sheep*).

Pronouns

Pro means "for": a pronoun stands for a noun. Pronouns consist of a specifically limited group, most of which you'll find in this chapter. It's easy to bring a new noun into English: when a new object (such as the Internet) appears, we have to call it something, and whatchamacallit doesn't work for long. But we use pronouns so much that we are suspicious of new ones. Attempts to invent a nonsexist pronoun, for example by combining *he* and *she* with a hyphen or slash mark, have, for the most part, just created a new source of friction about gender issues.

We divide pronouns into nine categories:

- personal,
- possessive,
- reflexive,
- intensive,
- relative,
- interrogative,
- demonstrative,
- indefinite,
- and reciprocal.

(If you sang this list to the tune of "The Twelve Days of Christmas," it would go ". . . five golden rela-

tives, four interrogatives interrogating, three demon-
stratives demonstrating, two definites defining, and a
personal in a pear tree.")

Personal pronouns that refer to people or things
have three characteristics:

- singular or plural number;
- first, second, or third person (yourself, the person you're talking to, or the person you're referring to);
- subject or object case (*I, we, he, she,* and *they* are
  subject case; *me, us, him, her,* and *them* are object
  case; *you* and *it* serve as both subject and object
  cases).

		Singular	*Plural*
1st person	Subject	I	we
	Object	me	us
2nd person	Subject	you	you
	Object	you	you
3rd person	Subject	he, she, it	they
	Object	him, her, it	them

If the pronoun system of number, person, and
case seems complex, consider that English also used
to distinguish formal and familiar pronouns. *Thou*
was used to address people informally or intimately,
while *you* was reserved for formal or respectful address. It's a pity that we lost *thou.* Now we have to use
you for friends and enemies, grownups and children,
people and animals, superiors and subordinates.
That's more democratic, which is why it's less fun.

Possessive pronouns are adjectives that show owner-
ship or relationship.

Singular   my, mine, your, yours, her, hers, his,
           its

Plural   our, ours, your, yours, their, theirs

Intensive and reflexive pronouns are formed by
adding -*self* or -*selves* to a pronoun.

- Intensive pronouns stress the noun's action.

  Gandalf himself will bring the guest.

- Reflexive pronouns always reflect back on the
  performer of the action

The *queen* will disguise *herself* as a commoner when she shops at the mall.

Relative pronouns (*who, whom, whose, which, that*) introduce adjective clauses.

The alien beings *who* are pictured in movies such as *Alien* and novels such as *Ender's Game* play on our phobias of slimy, crawly things.

Interrogative pronouns (*who, whom, whose, which, that*) are used in questions.

Mirror, mirror on the wall, *who* is fairest of them all?

Demonstrative pronouns (*this, that, these, those*) point to or identify nouns.

Do *those* clear plastic aerobics shoes belong to Cinderella?

Indefinite pronouns (*all, another, any, anybody, anyone, both, each, either, everybody, few, many, most, neither, nobody, none, one, several, some, somebody, someone, something*) refer to unknown or unidentified nouns.

Does *anyone* think that shoe size is a strange criterion for choosing a mate?

The noun a pronoun stands for is its antecedent (literally, the word means "go before").

The *hobbit* had missed *his* supper entirely.

Reciprocal pronouns identify individuals in a plural antecedent.

R2D2 and C3PO gripe at *each other* like my Mom and Dad.

Adjectives

Adjectives (and articles) give information about, modify (limit, qualify, or specify) a noun or pronoun. An adjective or article can describe, point to, or tell how many.

Soft sunlight streams through *the* window in St. Paul's Cathedral every day.

Adjectives come before the words they modify unless they follow a linking verb.

She's a monster without being a myth, which is hardly *fair*.

Articles are sometimes classified as adjectives because they point to nouns and pronouns. There are only three: *a, an,* and *the*. If you've ever seen a sign that said something like "ye olde curiousity shoppe," you may wonder if there was once a fourth article, "ye." Actually that word is spelled with a letter we no longer use, called the "thorn." It looked rather like a Y, but it was pronounced "th." Read "ye" as *the*. Go ahead and poke a little fun at people who don't know better.

Verbs

Verbs tell what happens, what has happened, or what will happen; a few verbs (e.g., *is, seems*) simply show existence. In a sentence, the main verb can have one or more parts.

Indiana Jones *drew* his pistol and *shot* the swordsman.

As the scene was originally written, Indy *was going* to use a sword, but he *was* sick with an intestinal condition I won't detail.

Main verbs can be identified because they will change form in the following patterns:

Base form	Often I *sing*.
-s form	Often he *sings*.
Past tense	Yesterday I *sang*.
Past participle	I *have sung* this song.
Present participle	I *am singing* at the club next Friday night.

Regular verb forms have past tenses and past participles that are identical (*planned, planned*). If these forms are different (*went, gone*), the verb is irregular. English once had many more irregular verbs, but we have lost sight of those that are used less frequently than, for example, *go*. Many of the old irregular verbs have been regularized, that is, changed to conform to the pattern of verbs such as *walk*.

The verb *be* has eight forms:

- be (base),
- am,

- is,
- are (present),
- was,
- were (past),
- being,
- been (present and past participles).

Auxiliary (sometimes called "helping") verbs combine with main verbs to create tenses and aspects of verbs.

Ulysses *will be sailing* for Troy tomorrow, given his marital situation.

Confusion for ESL speakers occurs when particles function as part of the verb: *call on, be off, done in, go with.* These are idiomatic in English, and each functions according to its own delightfully individual history (imagine you hear peals of giddy laughter as you read this). You aren't delighted? Then you feel the way English speakers feel when they learn German, which has prefixes that are as eccentric as little old college professors. Take advice from Melancthon, and sin boldly. Use the particles as well as you can, and accept correction patiently.

Adverbs

Adverbs

- modify (limit, qualify, intensify, or specify) verbs, adjectives, or other adverbs

  It was *slightly* odd to see an elephant carrying a *mostly* naked man.
- tell how, where, or when

  Tarzan slid *easily* to the ground, avoiding chafing and splinters.
- show condition or degree

  He stood *very* quietly waiting for the animals to assemble.
- sometimes modify a whole sentence rather than any single part

  Naturally, hostile human eyes of assorted colors were observing him.

Conjunctions

Conjunctions connect words, phrases, and clauses, showing relationships between and among them.

- Coordinating conjunctions (*and, but, for, or, nor, so, yet*) connect equal elements.
- Correlative conjunctions (*either . . . or, neither . . . nor, not only . . . but also, whether . . . or, both . . . and*) work in pairs, also connecting equal elements.
- Subordinating conjunctions (*after, although, because, before, if, that, though, unless, until, when, where, whether, while*) show the relation of subordinate clauses to the rest of a sentence.
- Conjunctive adverbs (*accordingly, besides, certainly, consequently, finally, furthermore, however, instead, meanwhile, moreover, nevertheless, nonetheless, specifically, subsequently, therefore, thus*) show relationships between coordinating clauses.

Prepositions

Prepositions (*about, above, across, after, against, along, among, around, at, before, behind, below, beneath, beside, between, by, down, for, from, in, inside, into, of, on, out, over, to, toward, under, up, with, within, without*) connect nouns and pronouns to some other word, showing a relationship between or among the words. The preposition plus the noun or pronoun is called a prepositional phrase. These phrases function in a sentence as an adjective or an adverb.

In the beginning only animals *with fins* lived *in the sea.*

The prepositional phrase "In the beginning," functions as an adverb telling when; "with fins" functions as an adjective describing animals; "in the sea" functions as an adverb telling where they lived.

Prepositions

- comprise a rather large, though limited, group of words. We don't borrow or invent new prepositions as we do nouns and verbs.
- usually show direction or position. A helpful teacher of ours once observed that prepositions

indicate places a cat can go; a smart-aleck student in that class (we won't say who) added, in a stage whisper, "Yeah, right, places a cat can go, and captions for the illustrations in the *Kama Sutra.*"

- are used idiomatically in a way that causes difficulties for ESL speakers and even for native speakers at times. All writers should double-check prepositions in a usage dictionary.

Groups of words such as "along with" or "next to" are also sometimes classified as prepositions.

Interjections

Not really a "part" of a sentence, interjections are words or phrases that express strong emotion or surprise (*Oh no! Wow! Eek!*). They are often followed by an exclamation point. Comic book writers love to invent new interjections (*Aaargh! Unnnnggggg!*).

Parts of a Sentence

The word *sentence* comes from a Latin word meaning "a way of thinking or feeling." A sentence expresses thoughts, feelings, or actions performed by someone. The subject is the person, thing, word, or idea acting, being acted on, or existing. The predicate includes the verb with all its modifiers.

Subjects

The simple subject of a sentence includes the noun or pronoun performing the action of the verb. The complete subject includes all the modifiers with the noun or pronoun.

Both African and Indian *elephants* live for many years, rather like your least favorite coworkers and relatives.

Compound subjects have more than one noun or noun phrase.

Books and *movies* used to stimulate my more sociopathic fantasies, but now *television* and the *Internet* are competing as well.

The placement of the subject is flexible. Many sentences begin with the subject, but readable and engaging writing includes many variations on the basic pattern.

Did *you* enjoy Joanne Woodward as a psychiatrist named Dr. Watson in *They Might Be Giants?*

Inverted sentences catch readers' attention and suggest interesting subtleties of meaning.

Delightful was the *effect* of a female Dr. Watson treating a delusional Sherlock Holmes.

Expletive clauses begin with *there* or *it*. The true subject of a sentence based on an expletive clause usually follows the verb.

There will be few *answers* to life's problems without humor.

Verbs

Verbs may be categorized as linking, transitive, or intransitive in relation to the objects or complements they can or cannot take.

- A linking verb indicates that the information in the sentence (other than the subject) will describe or rename the subject. Most often linking verbs are a form of the verb *to be.* They may also include *appear, become, feel, grow, look, make, prove, seem, smell, sound,* and *taste* when the word group following describes the subject.
- A verb that shows the subject performing an action or thinking a thought is said to be transitive (*trans-* means "carrying across").
- Intransitive verbs are verbs that do not carry over action.

Complements

When the subject complement renames the subject, it is a noun or pronoun.

What famous novel is the *one* you wish you could live in?

When the complement describes the subject, it is an adjective.

The colors in Lily's dress, like her SAT scores, are *brilliant.*

All the goddesses, regardless of their immortality and omnipotence, seemed *eager* for the prize labeled "For the Fairest."

Direct Objects

Nouns or pronouns directly receiving the action of transitive verbs function as direct objects.

Hilary's odd friends in The Society for Creative Anachronism plan a *jousting tournament* every year.

This sentence is in the active voice: that is, the subject, *The Society for Creative Anachronism,* is acting on the direct object, *jousting tournament.* This sentence can be changed to passive voice by moving the direct object to the subject position.

A *jousting tournament* is planned every year by Hilary's odd friends in The Society for Creative Anachronism.

Indirect Objects

The indirect object is the noun or pronoun for whom the action in a transitive sentence is done.

Please call *me* a cab.

Depending on the way you read the example, you might respond to this request with "Okay, you're a cab," or "Where do you want to go?" In the latter reading, the pronoun *me* functions as the indirect object, the person for whom the calling is done.

Passive   A cab must be called *for me.*

Note again that the direct object, in this case *cab,* becomes the subject in a passive sentence.

Object Complements

An object complement is a noun, adjective, or noun phrase or clause that completes the object's meaning.

Before women call each other *sister,* they usually call each other *everything else.*

Supper makes all horses *tame.*

Intransitive Verbs

Intransitive verbs take neither objects nor complements.

Time flies.

There *are* two ways to read this sentence, one with an intransitive verb and one with a transitive verb.

The intransitive sentence means "Time goes by quickly." If someone said, "Time flies," you might answer, "Yes, it does." No object or complement can follow the verb *flies* in this sentence.

The transitive sentence uses *time* as a verb meaning "to measure time," and the noun *flies* (i.e., winged insects) as the direct object. Transitive "Time flies" means "Determine how much time it takes for those flies to cover a certain distance." If someone ordered you to "Time flies," you might answer, "I can't time them. Flies fly too fast."

Clauses

Clauses and phrases function as parts of speech and as parts of a sentence. Clauses may be independent or dependent. This section discusses how the different word groups function in specific ways.

Noun clauses

Noun clauses function in the sentence where nouns or pronouns would function, as subjects, objects, or complements. They generally begin with *who, what, when, where,* or *why* or variations on these words.

Whatever you ask for will seem less appealing the minute you get it.

Adjective clauses

Adjective clauses function where an adjective would function in a sentence. These clauses begin with relative pronouns (*who, which, that*). They answer the questions *which* or *what kind?*

In teenage slasher movies, you always know it's the person wearing the least clothing *who will be the next victim.*

Adverb clauses

These clauses function as adverbs in a sentence, modifying verbs, adjectives, or other adverbs. They begin with subordinating conjunctions (*after, although, as, because, before, if, since, though, unless, until, when, where, whether, while*). They tell you *when, where, why,* or *how.*

> *As he was led into the forest by his creepy parents,* Hansel left a trail of bread crumbs.

> I've always suspected he knew that the route home would be lost *when birds ate the crumbs.*

Phrases

Phrases are groups of words that do not have a subject and verb.

Verbal phrases

Verbal phrases include a form of a verb that does not function as a part of a clause. Possible verbal phrases are infinitive phrases (*to* and a form of a verb, such as *to go* or *to have*) and participial phrases (present: *-ing* form of the verb, such as *going, having*; past: *-ed, -t, -n* form of the verb, such as *gone, had*).

Infinitive phrases   Infinitive phrases function as adjectives, adverbs, or nouns.

> The weapon *to be used in quaint, old-fashioned wars* is a longbow.

> Sir Luke killed a perfectly nice dragon *to please the whiny maiden.*

> We want to live long enough *to become a problem to our children.*

Participial phrases   Participial phrases always function as adjectives.

> *Seizing the opportunity and the microphone,* the shrill soprano sang the anthem.

> *Faced with a choice between two evils,* choose the one you haven't tried before.

Gerund phrases

Since gerund phrases fill slots that nouns can occupy, it's easy to see that they function as nouns.

Here the gerund serves as the subject.

Giving students impossible assignments is often fun.

Here the gerund serves as the direct object.

Captain Kirk regretted *scolding Commander Spock.*

Prepositional phrases

Prepositional phrases include a preposition that shows a relationship to a noun or pronoun. The prepositional phrase functions as an adjective or an adverb.

Functioning as adjective	The ram *in the thicket* saved Isaac.
Functioning as adverb	The fox ran *into the thicket.*

Appositive phrases

Appositive phrases immediately follow and rename a noun or pronoun.

Dana Scully, *the FBI agent,* often worked nights and weekends.

Absolute phrases

Absolute phrases modify whole clauses or sentences. They have a noun and a verb but are not clauses themselves.

Her partner having been kidnapped by aliens, she is spending this weekend at the beach.

Absolute phrases are easy to mistake for clauses because they contain a subject and a form of the verb. The clue is that the verb includes an *-ing* and is unaffected when the apparent subject changes from singular to plural. Try adding an *-s* to partner in the sample sentence. The verb form "having been kidnapped" remains the same. A word to the wise (and especially to travelogue narrators): absolute phrases that aren't watched closely may lose their heads, steal away, and become unruly dangling modifiers.

Further Reference

If you've double-checked the table of contents and index and still find that the question you're asking doesn't seem to be handled in this book, you may need to locate some of the books we use when we need answers.

Sentences

Christensen, Francis and Bonniejean Christensen. *Notes Toward a New Rhetoric: Nine Essays for Teachers*. 2nd ed. New York: Harper, 1978.

McCrorie, Ken. *Telling Writing*. 4th ed. Upper Montclair: Boynton/Cook, 1985.

Strunk, W., and E. B. White. *The Elements of Style*. 4th ed., Boston: Allyn & Bacon, 2000.

Williams, Joseph M. *Style: Toward Clarity and Grace*. Chicago: U of Chicago P, 1995.

Words

Follett, Wilson. *Modern American Usage: A Guide*. Ed. and comp. Jacques Barzun, with Carlos Baker et al. New York: Avenel, 1980.

Fowler, H. W. *The New Fowler's Modern English Usage*. 3rd ed. Ed. R. W. Burchfield. Oxford: Clarendon Press; New York: Oxford UP, 1996.

Merriam Webster's Dictionary of English Usage. Springfield: Merriam-Webster, Inc., 1994.

The Oxford English Dictionary. 2nd ed. 1991.

Webster's Third New International Dictionary of the English Language. Unabridged. 1993.

Punctuation and Mechanics

Judd, Karen. *Copyediting, a Practical Guide.* 2nd ed. Los Altos: Crisp, 1990.

The Chicago Manual of Style. 14th ed. Chicago: U of Chicago P, 1993.

Documentation

Gibaldi, Joseph. *MLA Handbook for Writers of Research Papers.* 5th ed. New York: Modern Language Association of America, 1995.

Turabian, Kate L. *A Manual for Writers.* 6th ed. U of Chicago P, 1996.

Publication Manual of the American Psychological Association. 4th ed. Washington, DC: APA, 1994.

Grammar and Language

Greenbaum, Sidney, and Randolph Quirk. *A Student's Grammar of the English Language.* Harlow: Longman, 1990.

Millward, Celia M. *A Biography of the English Language.* 2nd ed. Fort Worth: Harcourt, 1996.

APPENDIX

2

A Little Usage Test

Directions: First, warm up by reading the beginning (49–59) of Chapter 2, "A Few Words About Words," and doing a quick set of hamstring stretches. Then run through the following silly little essay, looking for questionable word choices based on Chapter 2's four categories of usage issues: Important Idioms, Dangerous Pairs, Tricky Changes, and Inappropriate Tones. Let's say that there are, oh, twenty of them, five for each category. The questionable choices appear in the essay minus any identifying marks, just as they would in real life, so that you have to find the questions in order to figure out the answers (pretend you're on an Easter egg hunt). Some of the items are listed in Chapter 2's usage glossary (59–70), and some aren't, so that you have to use the categories to identify possible usage questions (okay, that's not fair, but just get over it).

You get full credit for knowing which words and phrases are questionable, double credit for knowing what the correct choice is, and triple credit for knowing you need to refer to a usage dictionary to confirm your opinion. Failing to look everything up costs you all the points you have gained.

Life Not Only Begins at Forty, It Begins to Show.

Jokes rely on a punch line, a statement that contrasts in content or style with the straight line, creating an affect of movement from a higher, soberer place to a lower, sillier place. The poet Alexander Pope used the term *bathos* to describe this movement. In the title joke above, the bathos involves a fall from a cheerful to a rueful attitude about middle age—from thoughts of liberty and affluence to thoughts of wrinkles and fat. Like a middle-aged person, humor achieves meaning with a serious beginning followed by a show of absurdity.

181

According to Sigmund Freud, jokes usually operate on our insecurities. Schoolchildren can illicit nervous laughter from well-socialized classmates by speaking obscenities aloud in class. More adult audiences require more subtle forms of bad behavior. Sensitive subjects such as age, sex, death, race, class, gender, ethnicity, region, and family create anxiety among adults, and that anxiety can power a joke. Even simple jokes rely on the audience for complex cultural cross-referencing. "If you want breakfast in bed, sleep in the kitchen." The one-liner is orientated toward an audience that is female, middle-class, and domestic. The joke is female because serving meals is a social role that is gendered female; middle-class because traditional roles are likeliest to be contested in the middle class, where two-career households are an issue; and domestic because it implies both intimacy and conflict. The audience might hopefully find the joke funny because it expresses a sassy thought hidden in the minds of people who care for others in domestic situations.

Humorous writers develop a recognizable style by characteristic choices of subject matter or language. Erma Bombeck, for example, writes about domestic issues using a pattern of bathos that involves a high sentiment followed by a mundane event of family life. "All of us have moments in our lives that test our courage. Taking children into a house with white carpet is one of them." The common subject matter of domestic life sets a situation in which a wide audience can share consciousness with Erma's beleaguered house-wife persona.

Dave Barry, another newspaper humorist, uses a variation on Erma's pattern. While he also writes about everyday life, his bathos often stems from unpredictable word choices. Consider the way he describes baby boomers' views of their children, who will become "solid, productive citizens once they gain a little maturity, remove their body piercings, [and] start wearing normal-sized pants instead of what appear to be caterer's tents with pockets." The studied awkwardness of phrasing like "piercings" and "instead of what appear to be" encourage you to expect the strongly denotative word-choice of Barry's cartoon punch line: "caterer's tents with pockets."

Literary humorists require a literate audience, comprised of people who know literature and culture. In "The Literary Offenses of Fenimore Cooper," Mark Twain lampoons fellow novelist James Fenimore Cooper by juxtaposing Cooper's high (and sometimes overdone) novelistic style with the folksy vernacular style Twain invented for *Huckleberry Finn*. We are supposed to be amused when Twain moves from Cooperesque high style to Huckleberryesque low style that belies his scorn for Cooper.

In the following sample, Twain's low style is underlined, so that you can imagine yourself reading along and then stumbling over the line and falling on your nose when the tone changes. Double underlines signify that you would have to be a kangaroo not to stumble.

> For several years, Cooper was daily in the society of artillery, and he ought to have noticed that when a cannon-ball strikes the ground it either buries itself or skips a hundred feet or so; skips again a hundred feet or so—and so on, till finally it gets tired and rolls. Now in one place he loses some "females"—as he always calls women—in the edge of a wood near a plain at night in a fog, on purpose to give Bumppo a chance to show off the delicate art of the forest before the reader. These mislaid people are hunting for a fort. They hear a cannon-blast, and a cannon-ball presently comes rolling into the wood and stops at their feet. To the females this suggests nothing. The case is very different with the admirable Bumppo. I wish I may never know peace again if he doesn't strike out promptly and follow the track of that cannon-ball across the plain in the dense fog and find the fort. Isn't it a daisy?

The vernacular intrusions into nineteenth century novelistic idiom impact Cooper's grandiosity with a clever Yankee anti-stuffed-shirt humor.

Dorothy Parker's humorous poetry is based on inside jokes about her Bohemian life, her sophisticated use of verse forms, and her allusiveness.

"The Flaw in Paganism" is a joke about hangovers and other consequences of unconventional behavior—not a very subtle kind of humor. Irregardless, Parker's treatment appeals to an audience even more knowing than Twain's. She paraphrases the Biblical "eat and drink for tomorrow we die" (Isaiah xxii. 13) to create a straight line ("Drink and dance and laugh and lie . . ./For tomorrow we shall die!") and adds an ironic comment as punch line ("But, alas, we never do."), so that her pagan debauchery is emphasized by the moral overtones of a Biblical context. To terminate her witty tour de farce, she invents a verse form with a stress pattern that emphasizes her verbs.

"Words of Comfort to Be Scratched on a Mirror," which is also in the joke pattern of straight line and punch line, relies on a sequence of bad girls from history, beginning with Helen of Troy ("had a wandering glance"), who most people would know, and ending with Ninon ("was ever the chatter of France"), an infamous seventeenth century courtesan that most people would have to look up in an encyclopedia at this point in time. When Parker gets to the ironic punch line ("But oh, what a good girl am I!"), which is supposed to infer that she is an even more scandalous woman than the three so far named, the thought and phrasing create an elegant bathetic effect.

In general then, humor like water runs downhill, and when you get to the bottom, if the humor is deep enough, you can lie back, relax, and soak in the bathos.

Answers to the Little Usage Test

Look for boldfaced words that are followed by words in brackets. The former are the questionable usage and the latter are the appropriate replacements. The choices are categorized as follows.

- Important Idioms—who, that, hopefully, irregardless, utilize
- Dangerous Pairs—infer, illicit, comprised, belies, affect
- Tricky Changes—tour de farce, gendered, impact, orientated, like
- Inappropriate Tone—terminate, persona, minus, unconventional behavior, at this point in time.

Directions: First, warm up by reading the beginning (pp. 49–59) of Chapter 2, "A Few Words About Words," and doing a quick set of hamstring stretches. Then run through the following silly little essay, looking for questionable word choices based on Chapter 2's four categories of usage issues: Important Idioms, Dangerous Pairs, Tricky Changes, and Inappropriate Tones. Let's say that there are, oh, twenty of them, five for each category. The questionable choices appear in the essay **minus** [without] any identifying marks, just as they would in real life, so that you have to find the questions in order to figure out the answers (pretend you're on an Easter egg hunt). Some of the items are listed in Chapter 2's usage glossary (pp. 59–70), and some aren't, so that you have to **utilize** [use] the categories to identify possible usage questions (okay, that's not fair, but just get over it).

You get full credit for knowing which words and phrases are questionable, double credit for knowing what the correct choice is, and triple credit for knowing you need to refer to a usage dictionary to confirm your opinion. Failing to look everything up costs you all the points you have gained.

Life Not Only Begins at Forty, It Begins to Show.

Jokes rely on a punch line, a statement that contrasts in content or style with the straight line, creating an **affect** [effect] of movement from a higher, soberer place to a lower, sillier place. The poet Alexander Pope used the term *bathos* to describe this movement. In the title joke above, the bathos involves a fall from a cheerful to a rueful attitude about middle age—from thoughts of liberty and affluence to thoughts of wrinkles and fat. Like a middle-aged person, humor achieves meaning with a serious beginning followed by a show of absurdity.

According to Sigmund Freud, jokes usually operate on our insecurities. Schoolchildren can **illicit** [elicit] nervous laughter from well-socialized classmates by speaking obscenities aloud in class. More adult audiences require more subtle forms of bad behavior. Sensitive subjects such as age, sex, death, race, class, gender, ethnicity, region, and family create anxiety among adults, and that anxiety can power a joke. Even simple jokes rely on the audience for complex cultural cross-referencing. "If you want breakfast in bed, sleep in the kitchen." The one-liner **is orientated toward** [relies on] an audience that is female, middle-class, and domestic. The joke is female because serving meals is a social role that is **gendered** [stereotypically] female; middle-class because traditional roles are likeliest to be contested in the middle class, where two-career households are an issue; and domestic because it implies both intimacy and conflict. The audience might **hopefully** [DELETE] find the joke funny because it expresses a sassy thought hidden in the minds of people who care for others in domestic situations.

Humorous writers develop a recognizable style by characteristic choices of subject matter or language. Erma Bombeck, for example, writes about domestic issues using a pattern of bathos that involves a high sentiment followed by a mundane event of family life. "All of us have moments in our lives that test our courage. Taking children into a house with white carpet is one of them." The common subject matter of domestic life sets a situation in which a wide audience can share consciousness with Bombeck's beleaguered housewife **persona** [DELETE].

Dave Barry, another newspaper humorist, uses a variation on Bombeck's pattern. While he also writes about everyday life, his bathos often stems from unpredictable word choices. Consider the way he describes baby boomers' views of their children, who will become "solid, productive citizens once they gain a little maturity, remove their body piercings, [and] start wearing normal-sized pants instead of what appear to be caterer's tents with pockets." The studied awkwardness of phrasing **like** [such as] "piercings" and "instead of what appear to be" encourage you to expect the strongly denotative word-choice of Barry's cartoon punch-line: "caterer's tents with pockets."

Literary humorists require a literate audience, **comprised** [composed] of people who know literature and culture. In "The Literary Offenses of Fenimore Cooper," Mark Twain lampoons fellow novelist James Fenimore Cooper by juxtaposing Cooper's high (and sometimes overdone) novelistic style with the folksy vernacular style Twain invented for Huckleberry Finn. We are supposed to be amused when Twain moves from Cooperesque high style to Huckleberryesque low style that **belies** [betrays] his scorn for Cooper.

In the following sample, Twain's low style is underlined, so that you can imagine yourself reading along and then stumbling over the line and falling on your nose when the tone changes. Double underlines signify that you would have to be a kangaroo not to stumble.

> For several years, Cooper was daily in the society of artillery, and he ought to have noticed that when a cannon-ball strikes the ground it either buries itself or skips a hundred feet or so; skips again a hundred feet or so—and so on, till finally it <u>gets tired and rolls</u>. <u>Now in one place he loses some "females"—as he</u>

always calls women—in the edge of a wood
near a plain at night in a fog, <u>on purpose</u> to
give Bumppo a chance to show off the deli-
cate art of the forest before the reader. These
<u>mislaid</u> people are hunting for a fort. They
hear a cannon-blast, and a cannon-ball
presently comes rolling into the wood and
stops at their feet. To the females this suggests
nothing. The case is very different with the
admirable Bumppo. <u>I wish I may never know
peace again if he doesn't</u> strike out promptly
and follow the track of that cannon-ball
across the plain in the dense fog and find the
fort. <u>Isn't it a daisy?</u>

The vernacular intrusions into nineteenth
century novelistic idiom **impact** [ridicule]
Cooper's grandiosity with a clever Yankee anti-
stuffed-shirt humor.

Dorothy Parker's humorous poetry is based on
inside jokes about her Bohemian life, her sophisticated use of verse forms, and her allusiveness.

"The Flaw in Paganism" is a joke about hangovers and other consequences of **unconventional
behavior** [debauchery]—not a very subtle kind of
humor. **Irregardless,**[But] Parker's treatment
appeals to an audience even more knowing than
Twain's. She paraphrases the Biblical "eat and
drink for tomorrow we die" (Isaiah xxii. 13) to
create a straight line ("Drink and dance and
laugh and lie . . ./For tomorrow we shall die!")
and adds an ironic comment as punch line ("But,
alas, we never do."), so that her pagan debauchery is emphasized by the moral overtones of a
Biblical context. To **terminate** [end] her witty
tour de **farce** [force], she invents a verse form
with a stress pattern that emphasizes her verbs.

"Words of Comfort to Be Scratched on a Mirror,"
which is also in the joke pattern of straight line
and punch line, relies on a sequence of bad girls
from history, beginning with Helen of Troy ("had
a wandering glance"), **who** [whom] most people
would know, and ending with Ninon ("was ever
the chatter of France"), an infamous seventeenth
century courtesan **that** [whom] most people

would have to look up in an encyclopedia **at this point in time** [DELETE]. When Parker gets to the ironic punch line ("But oh, what a good girl am I!"), which is supposed to **infer** [imply] that she is an even more scandalous woman than the three so far named, the thought and phrasing create an elegant bathetic effect.

In general then, humor like water runs downhill, and when you get to the bottom, if the humor is deep enough, you can lie back, relax, and soak in the bathos.

APPENDIX
4

Another Little Grammar Test

If you want to try another grammar test, count the clauses in this passage.

> Writers who are able to express their thoughts clearly and correctly may be unable to distinguish a dependent clause from one of Santa's tax exemptions. Pressed to define the term *dependent clause,* writers who are not grammarians may recall some comforting falsehood they think a grammarian has taught them. "Oh, that's easy. A dependent clause is—ummm—less important than an independent clause." Ask a grammarian to define a dependent clause, and he or she will name the parts of a sentence (subject and at least one finite verb) required to make a clause; distinguish a dependent from an independent clause, identifying both subordinating and coordinating conjunctions; and produce examples of independent and dependent clauses. Writers who are not grammarians will understand for a moment, but if the grammar lecture continues, they will grow as drowsy as Dorothy in the field of poppies.

You should have found 16 clauses.

Answers to the Little Grammar Tests

Brackets indicate clause boundaries.

Test 1

[¹Grammar and mythology operate the same way:] [²they both provide a system of names] [³that helps people to discuss and control the world of the mind.] [⁴The people [⁵who created the classical pantheon of gods and goddesses] were naming forces] [⁶they perceived in the world and in themselves.] [⁷External realities such as trees and rivers became ideas such as nymphs and minor gods,] [⁸while internal realities such as love and anger became more important deities, Venus and Mars.] By naming external and internal realities, [⁹the authors of classical mythology gained the ability to think and talk about the world in familiar terms,] [¹⁰which is a kind of control.] [¹¹Similar control is achieved] [¹²when people use terms such as *noun* and *verb* to achieve a sense of control over the language] [¹³they use.] Coincidentally, [¹⁴classical mythology and grammar come to us from the same sources]: Greek and Latin texts written before the Middle Ages. [¹⁵The same scholars [¹⁶who revived classical learning during the Renaissance] used the Latin grammar] [¹⁷they knew] in order to write an English grammar: to discuss, analyze, and, [¹⁸they hoped,] to control the development of English.

Test 2

[¹Writers [²who are able to express their thoughts clearly and correctly] may be unable to distinguish a dependent clause from one of Santa's tax exemptions]. Pressed to define the term *dependent clause,* [³such writers will probably recall some comforting falsehood] [⁴they think] [⁵they remember from school.][⁶"Oh, that's easy]. [⁷A dependent clause is—ummm—less important than an independent clause."] [⁸A writer [⁹who experiences the serene certainty] [¹⁰that only ignorance can produce] may cling to misleading oversimplifications of grammar]. [¹¹Ask a grammarian to define a dependent clause] and [¹²he or she will name the parts of a sentence (subject and at least one finite verb) required to make a clause; distinguish a dependent from an independent clause, identifying both subordinating and coordinating conjunctions; and produce some examples of independent and dependent clauses]. [¹³Writers [¹⁴who are not grammarians] will understand for a moment], but [¹⁵if the grammar lecture continues], [¹⁶they will grow]as drowsy as Dorothy in the field of poppies.

APPENDIX

6

Glossary of Grammatical Terms

Parts of Speech

Nouns

Nouns give names to

- persons, places, and things, such as *father, Greece,* and *candle*
- abstractions, such as *love, belief,* and *goddess*

Pronouns

- stand for nouns
- are a limited group, unlike nouns
- can be divided into nine categories (personal, possessive, reflexive, intensive, relative, interrogative, demonstrative, indefinite, and reciprocal), each with its own characteristics

Adjectives

- give information about, modify (limit, qualify, or specify), a noun or pronoun
- can describe, point to, or tell how many

Verbs

- tell what happens, what has happened, or what will happen
- sometimes simply show existence (e.g., *is, seems*)
- can have one or more parts (e.g., *races, was raced, will have been raced*)

Adverbs

- modify (limit, qualify, or specify) verbs, adjectives, or other adverbs

- tell how, where, or when
- show condition or degree

Conjunctions

- connect words, phrases, and clauses, showing relationships between and among them
- can be divided into four categories (coordinating conjunctions, correlative conjunctions, subordinating conjunctions, and conjunctive adverbs), each with its own characteristics

Prepositions

- connect nouns and pronouns to some other word, showing a relationship between or among the words
- combine with a noun or pronoun to form a prepositional phrase
- function in a sentence as an adjective or an adverb

Interjections

- are words and phrases, not really part of a sentence, that express strong feeling (*Ouch! Eeeww! Yay! Duhh!*)

Parts of a Sentence

Sentences

- consist of at least one subject and predicate

Subjects

- consist of at least one noun phrase

Noun Phrases

- consist of a noun and its modifiers

Predicates

- consist of at least one verb phrase

Verb Phrases

- consist of at least one verb and its modifiers

Verbs

- consist of at least one finite verb (i.e., a verb that changes its form to show singular or plural number, or past or future tense)

Objects

- consist of at least one noun or pronoun receiving the action of a verb

Complements

- consist of at least one noun, pronoun, adjective, noun phrase, noun clause, or adjective phrase that completes the meaning of a verb

APPENDIX 7

Online References

General Reference

American Heritage Dictionary:
   <www.bartleby.com/61/>

Usage Dictionary: <www.bartleby.com/64/>

Quotations: <www.bartleby.com/63/>

The Bible: <www.bartleby.com/people/Bible.html>

Encyclopedias: <www.searchgateway.com/
   encyclop.htm>

Writing Labs

Online Writery <www.missouri.edu/~writery>

Purdue University Online Writing Lab
   <owl.english.purdue.edu>

ESL Sites

Dave's ESL Café <eslcafe.com>

Topics: An Online Magazine by and for Learners
   of English <www.rice.edu/projects/topics/
   Electronic/Magazine.html>

Virtual Libraries

The Internet Public Library <ipl.org>

The WWW Virtual Library <vlib.org>

The Webliography: Internet Subject Guides
   <www.lib.lsu.edu/weblio.html>

Text Archives

Electronic Text Center—University of Virginia
    Library <etext.lib.virginia.edu/eng-on.html>

Bartleby.com on line <bartleby.com/>

Project Gutenberg <promo.net/pg>

Government Sites

U.S. Census Bureau: The Official Statistics
    <www.census.gov>

Thomas: Legislative Information on the Internet
    <thomas.loc.gov>

U.S. State & Local Gateway <www.statelocal.gov>

U.S. Government Printing Office
    <www.access.gpo.gov>

United Nations <www.un.org>

News Sites

The New York Times on the Web
    <www.nytimes .com>

The Washington Post <www.washingtonpost.com>

U.S. News Online <www.usnews.com/usnews/
    home.htm>

nationalgeographic.com
    <www.nationalgeographic.com/mai.html>

CNN Interactive <www.cnn.com>

Newsgroups and Listservs

Tile.Net <www.tile.net>

Liszt <www.liszt.com>

Deja News <www.dejanews.com>

Sites for Evaluating Sources

Evaluating Web Sites: Criteria and Tools, Olin
    Kroch Uris Libraries
    <www.library.cornell.edu/
    okuref/research/webeval.html>

Evaluating Internet Resources, Milner Library,
    Illinois State University <www.mlb.ilstu.edu/
    ressubj/subject/intrnt/evaluate.htm>

COMPUTER TIP

Use the style and wizard functions to format business documents.

- Your word-processing program will provide templates with varying levels of formality to help you get started with documents such as memos, business letters, and resumes.

Grading Symbols

The table that follows contains a short list of remarks and symbols you don't want to find in anything you have written. Whether in red ink or black, these are warning signs that you ignore at considerable peril.

- Refer to the table to interpret marginal comments identifying problems in papers your instructor has marked.

- Refer to the pages indicated to find advice on solving the problems, keep track of the problems that recur in subsequent papers, and get help from your instructor or writing center if you need it.

- You and all your readers will find it very restful when these symbols cease to appear in your margins

Grading Symbols

Grading Symbol (and page number)	Explanation of Problem	Problem in Context	Correction
abb (108–110)	inappropriate abbreviation	In ~~exams~~, those who do not wish to know ask questions of those who cannot tell.	In examinations, those who do not wish to know ask questions of those who cannot tell.
awk (k) (see your instructor)	an awkward construction that may correspond to any of the grading symbols	When language or space ~~are insufficiently~~ to ~~their~~ frustration, a teacher ~~write~~ "awk" or "k" in the margin in ~~their~~ despair.	A teacher may write "awk" or "k" in the margin when language or space is insufficient to express her despair.
case (35, 166–169)	confusion between subject and object case in pronoun form	It was ~~hers~~ who said that as one gets older, the pickings get slimmer; but the people don't.	It was she who said that as one gets older, the pickings get slimmer; but the people don't.
cs (40–42)	comma used to splice two independent clauses together	I am in ~~shape, round~~ is a shape.	I am in shape; round is a shape.
dm (12–13)	modifier that "dangles," i.e., has no logical referent in the sentence	~~Running down the hill~~, my nose began to itch.	As I was running down the hill, my nose began to itch.
frag (39)	fragmentary sentence	We all have photographic ~~memories. But~~ don't all have film.	We all have photographic memories, but we don't all have film.

204

Code	Description	Example (with errors)	Corrected
fs (40–42)	two clauses fused into one sentence with incorrect punctuation	There are two tragedies in life. One is to lose your heart's ~~desire the~~ other is to gain it.	There are two tragedies in life. One is to lose your heart's desire; the other is to gain it.
irreg (27–28)	irregular verb form	To annoy Mother, I ~~lay~~ on the couch and ~~set~~ on the kitchen counter.	To annoy Mother, I lie on the couch and sit on the kitchen counter.
jarg (56)	inappropriate use of technical language	~~BEV~~ speakers routinely ~~eschew copulatives~~ in ~~utterances~~ such as "He is ready."	Speakers of Black English usually drop the verb is from a sentence such as "He is ready."
mix (10–11)	mixed construction	~~Just because~~ we got into this mess stupidly doesn't mean we can't get out the same way.	That we got into this mess stupidly doesn't mean we can't get out the same way.
mm (12–13)	misplaced modifier	Always suspect any job men vacate for women ~~willingly~~.	Always suspect any job men willingly vacate for women.
mood (30)	incorrect form of the verb for a command or hypothetical statement	He was so incompetent as a teacher that we insisted he ~~was~~ promoted to administration.	He was so incompetent as a teacher that we insisted he be promoted to administration.
pass (20–21)	passive form of verb where active form is preferable	What ~~is learned~~ from history is that nothing ~~can be learned~~ from history.	We learn from history that we learn nothing from history.

(continued)

Grading Symbol (and page number)	Explanation of Problem	Problem in Context	Correction
person (8–9, 32)	use of <u>you</u> where <u>one</u> is required	Take a big step if you need to. ~~You~~ cannot cross a chasm in two small jumps.	<u>Take a big step if you need to. One cannot cross a chasm in two small jumps.</u>
pn agr (31–32)	use of plural pronoun where singular is required	No one who is paid by the word can afford to be careless with ~~their~~ hyphens.	<u>Those who</u> are paid by the word must be careful with <u>their</u> hyphens.
ref (32–33)	unclear relationship between a pronoun and the noun it stands for	Parents can always depend on children to quote ~~them~~ correctly when ~~they~~ have said something ~~they~~ shouldn't have.	Parents <u>who say something they shouldn't have</u> can always depend on children to quote them correctly.
run-on (40–42)	two or more clauses run together with incorrect punctuation	Love is ~~grand divorce~~ is a hundred grand.	Love is <u>grand: divorce</u> is a hundred grand.
sexist (7–8)	word choice that creates unnecessary or prejudicial distinctions based on gender	You can always recognize a well-informed ~~man~~ because ~~he~~ shares your views.	You can always recognize well-informed <u>people</u> because <u>they</u> share your views.
slang (56)	inappropriate use of popular language	I'm all about ~~gibs~~ with this ~~phat GPU~~ and ~~DDR SDRAM~~.	I get great blood-and-guts effects in my video games because my video card has a lot of memory.

sp (see a dictionary)	spelling error	If we see you smoking, we'll assume ~~your~~ on fire and take appropriate action.	If we see you smoking, we'll assume you're on fire and take appropriate action.
sv agr (21–27)	subject verb agreement—both must be either singular or plural	Communism, like other revealed religions, ~~are~~ largely made up of prophecies.	Communism, like other revealed religions, is largely made up of prophecies.
t (28–30)	any of various problems with verb tense	We decided to continue the beatings until the morale ~~was~~ improved.	We decided to continue the beatings until the morale had been improved.
v (30–31)	misuse of active or passive voice	Difficulties ~~are made by~~ some people, and difficulties ~~make~~ some people.	Some people make difficulties, and some people are made by difficulties.
w (1–2)	wordy	~~In fact, it is the~~ conscience that hurts when everything else feels so good.	Conscience hurts when everything else feels good.
// (13–15)	parallel ideas require parallel structures	Reduce complexity in daily living so that important thoughts and values can be brought into focus.	Simplify, simplify, simplify.
x (ask your grandma)	obvious error	If it ~~aint~~ broke, fix it till it is.	If it isn't broken, fix it till it is.

Index